TRUMPED
UP

ALAN DERSHOWITZ

BOMBARDIER
BOOKS

Post Hill
PRESS

A BOMBARDIER BOOKS BOOK
An Imprint of Post Hill Press

Trumped Up:
How Criminalization of Political Differences Endangers Democracy
© 2017 by Alan Dershowitz
All Rights Reserved

Cover Design by Quincy Avilio

Post Hill Press
New York • Nashville
posthillpress.com

This volume is dedicated to the shrinking number of true civil libertarians who place more importance on the rights and liberties of all Americans than on the partisan benefits of distorting the law to target political enemies.

CONTENTS

AN UNPRECEDENTED PRESIDENT

Donald Trump is the most unusual president in American history—and among the most provocative and controversial. We can't keep our eyes off him. His presence dominates the public discourse. His tweets become breaking news filling the 24/7 news cycle. He bluffs, blusters and baffles his opponents. His unique style has transformed not only campaign strategies, but the presidency itself. He is unlike anyone who has ever occupied the Oval Office. It is not surprising therefore, that his unprecedented actions raise unprecedented legal, constitutional, civil liberty and ethical issues. The Trump effect has led us into uncharted and dangerous territory. We may need a new jurisprudence to check our currently uncheckable chief executive. The framers of our constitutional system simply didn't contemplate a President Trump.

President Trump is spontaneous, unpredictable and uncontrollable. He comments in real time about ongoing events, despite efforts by his staff and lawyers to stop him. He insults his media detractors and political enemies and reacts to their insults and slights. He often seems to make decisions impulsively, without considering their longer-term implications. He has been careless with national security secrets and with facts. He shoots from the hip and often misses. These traits and others served him extremely well during the nominating process, separating him from the numerous grey politicians who also sought the presidential nomination. It also served him well, though perhaps slightly less well, during the general election, in which more Americans voted against him than for him, but in which more electors gave him the presidency.[1]

Now he is the President. And his unusual style serves him well in some instances and less well in others. He told the Russians secrets relating to anti-terrorist information gathering by our allies, including Israel. He has threatened to cut back on the First Amendment right of journalists

---

[1]   President Trump has alleged that voter irregularities denied him the popular vote, tweeting after the election that, "in addition to winning the Electoral College in a landslide, I won the popular vote if you deduct the millions of people who voted illegally." Trump has since created a commission to investigate his unproven allegations of massive voter fraud.

to criticize him while insisting on his right to criticize others. He has said and done things that resulted in several adverse court rulings by stating that he planned to ban Muslims from entering the U.S., he undermined his own temporary ban on people coming from a number of Muslim countries.

President Trump's statements and actions may have also resulted in the appointment of a special counsel to investigate actions allegedly undertaken by his administration. His own actions – firing FBI Director James Comey, having the White House attribute the firing to a memo written by Deputy Attorney General Rod Rosenstein, stating that he would have fired Comey without regard to the memo, and then conversing with Comey out of the presence of witnesses – all contributed to the decision by Rosenstein to appoint a special counsel. Comey leaked the contents of their communications in a calculated, and successful effort to have a special counsel appointed. Rosenstein selected a close friend and longtime professional colleague of Comey to be the special counsel. President Trump has understandably railed against being investigated for firing Comey by a friend and professional colleague of the former FBI director.

The appointment of the special counsel raises profound issues of constitutional law, criminal law, legal ethics and civil liberties. Can a sitting president be tried for a crime he may have committed while in office or during the campaign or transition? Can the president commit the crime of obstruction of justice by exercising his constitutional power to order the director of the FBI to end an investigation and then firing him for not doing so? Does the evidence in the case show a corrupt motive by the president? If it does, is that enough to turn innocent constitutionally authorized acts into crimes? If there was coordination between the Trump campaign and the Russians, would that be a crime? I will address these and other issues in the pages to come.

THE SPECIAL COUNSEL

The role of the special counsel should be limited to investigating and prosecuting violations of federal criminal statutes. The special counsel is not an ombudsman; he is not a private investigator; he is not a legislator filling gaps in existing laws; he is not a scientist searching for objective truth; he is not a political pundit commenting on political gaffs; and he is certainly not God deciding whether his subjects belong in heaven or hell. He is simply another prosecutor who, under our rule of law, should have a narrow jurisdiction.

Among the problems with a special counsel, as distinguished from a more usual prosecutor, is that the mandate of the special counsel is far more specific. He is given either a subject or a person to investigate. In this case the subject is, roughly speaking, the Russian connection: was there any collaboration between the Trump campaign and Russian officials in the run-up to the election and during the transition period? And if so, were any crimes committed? His target is the Trump administration, and his "White Whale" is Donald Trump. In Melville's great American novel *Moby Dick*, Captain Ahab was obsessed with one target: the gigantic white whale that had crippled him during a prior encounter. He must kill the whale even at the cost of his own life and that of his crew. Previous special prosecutors have also had specific targets, such as President Clinton and President Nixon. Both succeeded in uncovering evidence of wrongdoing that was beyond their original mandate: the former leading to an unsuccessful impeachment, and the latter to the only presidential resignation in American history.

Justice Department regulations provide for the Attorney General to decide when a special prosecutor is warranted, and who should be entrusted with that responsibility. However, in this instance, as Attorney General Jeff Sessions recused himself from any investigation into charges that Russia interfered in the 2016 presidential election (after he allegedly failed to disclose meetings he had with the Russian Ambassador in Washington) Robert Mueller was appointed special counsel by Deputy Attorney General Rod Rosenstein.

According to the memorandum released by Rosenstein, Mueller has the authority not only to investigate "any links and/or coordination between the Russian government and individuals associated with the campaign of Donald Trump," but also "any matters which arose or may arise directly from the investigation." The memorandum also referenced the Justice Department's regulation (section 600.4(a)), which authorizes the special counsel to probe any attempts to illegally thwart the investigation. While Rosenstein gave the special counsel authority to "prosecute federal crimes arising from the investigation of these matters," Mueller's mandate is limited and his key decision-making may be overseen by the Deputy Attorney General at any time.

The problem – among many – is that Rosenstein would be an important witness in any investigation that included the firing of James Comey, since Rosenstein wrote a memo justifying the firing. Conflicts of interest abound in this matter.

The selective leaking of details surrounding the Russia investigation – which may themselves be crimes – makes it difficult to keep track of precisely who and what are the subjects of the probe. What we do know is that the FBI began an investigation into alleged ties between the Trump campaign and Russia in July 2016, before the Republican National Convention took place in Cleveland. At this time, revelations began to emerge about reported ties between Carter Page, an early foreign policy advisor to candidate Trump, and Russia. Page had extensive business links in Russia and was reported to have shuffled back-and-forth to Moscow to meet with high-level Russian officials. He was fired in September. Around the same time details surfaced regarding the alleged connection between Trump's campaign manager Paul Manafort and high-level Russian officials. Manafort worked on behalf of a pro-Russian Ukrainian political party and lobbied on behalf of other Russian officials with close ties to the Kremlin. He was fired in August and is said to be at the center of the Justice Department's ongoing investigation. Meanwhile, a key ally and advisor to Trump during the campaign, Roger Stone – who forewarned in July 2016 that Wikileaks would continue to drop bombshells on the Clinton campaign – is also reported to be within the scope of the investigation.

Most revelations have focused on President Trump's former national security advisor General Michael Flynn, who was told by the Justice Department shortly after his appointment in November that he was under investigation for his undisclosed lobbying on behalf of Turkish officials. Flynn later lied to Vice President Pence about various communications he had with the Russian Ambassador regarding sanctions imposed on that country. It has also been reported that Flynn failed to disclose payments from Russia Today, a state-run television network widely considered a Putin propaganda channel. Flynn resigned from his post in February. Moreover, Attorney General Jeff Sessions was also said to have failed to disclose conversations he had with the Russian Ambassador in Washington D.C. before President Trump's inauguration, and subsequently recused himself from any investigation pertaining to charges that Russia interfered in the 2016 presidential election.

Most recently, the President's son-in-law and key advisor Jared Kushner was reported to have had undisclosed meetings with the Russian Ambassador in Washington, and also with a Russian banker with close ties to Putin. Kushner reportedly proposed establishing a direct communication line with the Russian government outside traditional diplomatic channels.

At the time of this writing, I have seen no evidence of any violation of federal criminal statutes by Trump or by any current members of his administration. But the absence of evidence is not always evidence of absence, and so it is possible that the special counsel will uncover some criminal violations, perhaps against General Michael Flynn or others, for failing to disclose entirely lawful contact with Russian officials during the campaign and transition periods.

Special Prosecutor Robert Mueller is not targeting President Trump – at least not yet. As a matter of law and fact, there is no current basis for regarding President Trump as a target of any prosecution. But prosecutors always seek the biggest and most visible target, if the facts and the law were to justify it. So I have little doubt that Robert Mueller and his investigators will try to subject President Trump and his White House staff to the legal equivalent of a colonoscopy. They will search everywhere and leave no stone unturned in an effort to determine whether criminality can be established. It may therefore be technically true that the President is not being investigated, but it may also be true that the broad-based investigation being conducted by Mueller will include actions taken by Trump.

PRESIDENT TRUMP'S STYLE AND SUBSTANCE

President Trump's unconventional communication style has both benefited him and gotten him into some trouble during the first months of his presidency. His extensive tweeting about the controversial "travel ban" following the terror attacks in London, led many to argue that he was hurting his own executive order which may ultimately be reviewed by the Supreme Court. President Trump tweeted: "The Justice Dept. should have stayed with the original Travel Ban, not the watered down, politically correct version they submitted to S.C," and in a separate tweet wrote: "People, the lawyers and the courts can call it whatever they want, but I am calling it what we need and what it is, a TRAVEL BAN!"

Many believe that these tweets will not bode well for the President who has already had his past statements – made both during the campaign and after – used against him in court where his orders were found unconstitutional. When I was asked by *Business Insider* whether these specific tweets will be of detriment to the President's case, I said that I did not think so because he didn't tweet the words "Muslim ban." It is, in fact, a "travel ban," albeit a temporary one. I added that I do not believe that President Trump's statements should be considered in assessing the executive order because "you can't judge a statute by what people say about it. You have to judge it by its words. And I think the Supreme Court will ultimately come to realize that." Under the reasoning of some lower courts, had the original executive order been issued by President Obama, it would have been constitutional. Yet, because President Trump issued it, it is unconstitutional. I discussed this slippery slope in my columns where I criticized, as "a bridge too far," the argument that "any executive order issued by President Trump dealing with travel from Muslim countries would be constitutionally suspect because of what candidate Trump said." This argument, in my view, "turns constitutional analysis into psychoanalysis, requiring that the motives of the president be probed."

The special counsel's broad investigation raises some dangerous implications for civil liberties. But the Trump administration has also endangered civil liberties during its first few months in office. Trump has tried to weaken constitutional protection accorded political speech. On the campaign trail, candidate Trump vowed to change libel laws to make it easier to sue his critics. This is what he said: "I'm going to open up our libel laws so when they write purposely negative and horrible and false articles, we can sue them and win lots of money." This campaign "pledge" has carried over into the White House, with administration officials affirming on TV that they are "still looking" into changing libel laws that would make it easier to sue media organizations for negative coverage of the Trump White House. But any such change could boomerang against Trump himself, who uses ad hominem attacks as a political weapon against his detractors and political opponents. Recall when he accused President Obama of "tapping my phones…just prior to election." Trump doubled down on this claim despite the intelligence community's agreement that there was no basis for such an accusation. And consider when candidate Trump propounded the conspiracy theory that the father of Ted Cruz – his political rival – had associations with the man who killed JFK. Fortunately for the open market place of political ideas, both speech critical of the president and speech critical of his opponents are safeguarded by the First Amendment, and weakening press freedom would likely require a constitutional amendment or several new Supreme Court appointments. Neither is likely to occur.

President Trump's executive order regarding travel to the U.S. by people from certain Muslim countries has been among the most contentious sticking points of his presidency to date. While the executive order is multi-faceted and complex – and should be appraised and analyzed as such – its original presentation raised serious constitutional and legal issues. The Trump administration's initial draft failed to distinguish between the constitutional rights of green card holders, and foreigners who have never been to the U.S. Green card holders are entitled to due process, while the rights of foreigners seeking to come to the United States are much more limited. It was within this contextual framework that the Ninth Circuit's opinion stated: "the Government has not shown that the Executive Order provides what due process requires, such as notice and a hearing prior to an individual's ability to travel." By applying this order equally to individuals with different constitutional status, President Trump's "travel ban" – in its original incarnation – raised serious constitutional questions. However, the executive order has since been 'watered down,' and among its changes is the distinction between the rights of green card holders and those of other visitors to the United States. I believe that the Supreme Court is likely to find this redrafted order constitutional.

To vent his frustration with some courts blocking much of his executive orders, President Trump has resorted to aggressively attacking the judiciary, launching ad hominem tirades against judges whose decisions he disagrees with. When a Washington state federal judge temporarily blocked enforcement of his "travel ban," President Trump derided him as a "so called judge." Even Trump's Supreme Court nominee at the time, Neil Gorsuch, weighed in, calling such attacks on the judiciary "disheartening" and "demoralizing." Similarly, after the Trump administration's redrafted order was rebuked on appeal, Trump personally went after the credibility of the Ninth Circuit Court of Appeals, tweeting that it has "a terrible record of being overturned." And when a federal judge blocked Trump's executive order to withhold federal funding for "sanctuary cities," the White House released a statement saying this was an "egregious overreach by a single, unelected district judge." Such injudicious characterisations were also evident on the campaign trail when then candidate Trump aggressively attacked the judge in the now settled Trump University case, calling him "a hater." He then called for the judge to recuse himself because he is "Mexican," and therefore, according to Trump, could not neutrally preside over the litigation. The judge, whose family is of Mexican origin, is from Indiana.

Separation of powers and judicial independence are pillars of American democracy, and as a coequal branch of government, the judiciary serves as a check on the executive branch. The Trump administration's attempt to undermine the validity of the courts raises disturbing civil liberty issues.

President Trump has sometimes touted political or policy proposals that are hostile to civil liberties. He has broadly advocated giving "greater authority" to law enforcement, and has also called for widespread use of "stop-and-frisk" as a crime-fighting tool in inner-city neighborhoods. Moreover, in the context of addressing the increasing use of social media as a recruitment tool for terrorists, Trump offered a blanket proposal of "closing that internet up in some way." He continued to say, "somebody will say, 'Oh freedom of speech, freedom of speech. These are foolish people'" – offering no additional explanation for how this would be implemented in practice without violating basic rights of everyday Americans. And Trump has also advocated punishing flag burners either by putting them in jail or by taking away their citizenship. However, the Supreme Court has twice ruled that flag burning is protected under the First Amendment of the Constitution – as "symbolic speech" – and cannot be banned by the U.S. government. Nor can American citizens have their citizenship revoked, even as a punishment for crime.

TAKING SIDES

In our current age of hyper-partisan politics, nearly everyone takes sides. This is especially true with regard to the Trump presidency. It has become difficult to have a reasonable discussion about the most controversial president in our recent history. For Trump zealots, their president has not only committed no crimes, he has done nothing wrong. For anti-Trump zealots, nothing Trump has done – even in foreign policy – is good. Everything he has done is wrong, and since it is wrong it must necessarily be criminal. This deeply undemocratic fallacy – that political sins must be investigated and prosecuted as criminal – has been a pervasive mistake running through the media coverage of the Trump administration. Consider, for example, Tucker Carlson, a generally pro-Trump commentator on the generally pro-Trump Fox News. Carlson made the following observation when I said on his show that even if the Trump administration/ transition team knew that the Russians hacked the DNC or took advantage of that fact, it would not be a crime, unless they aided or abetted Russian crimes. Bemused, Carslon said: "I have been doing this almost every night for six months and I am embarrassed to admit that I have never thought about the point that you made, not one time. Why is there then a special counsel impanelled here?" I responded that perhaps there shouldn't be.

In a recent column for *The New York Times*, Roger Cohen described an encounter he had with Crystal Hesch – a liberal woman from Colorado – who since the election, has been struggling to find common ground with her father – an ardent Trump supporter. Cohen notes: "Hesch approached me in distress. She's frustrated that she can't even get to a point of departure for a reasoned discussion with her dad, a strong supporter of President Trump. 'What can I do? We can't even agree on a reality to discuss or a source we both accept,' she said. Like many Trump voters, her father is convinced there's a liberal plot to sabotage the president. Hesch's experience is normal. Tens of millions of Trump opponents cannot communicate with tens of millions of his supporters. There is no viable vocabulary. There is no shared reality." Cohen continued: "it's perhaps the most important problem confronting the United States, because the end point of hardening fracture and mutual incomprehension is violence."

Because of this hyper-partisan atmosphere, there has been little nuance in evaluating the behavior of President Trump and his administration. He either deserves the Nobel Prize, or he should be impeached, locked up and the key thrown away. To be sure, a handful of Republicans, led by Senators John McCain and Lindsey Graham have refused to defend all of Trump's conduct. But for the most part, the response of elected officials has been entirely predictable, following party lines. This has been the case especially since Republican candidates have won bi-elections after Trump took office.

The Trump election has hardened positions on both sides of the aisle, but the intolerance of the hard-left is far more prevalent on many university campuses where our future leaders are being educated. This trend has become even more troubling since the election of President Trump. CNN host, Fareed Zakaria, highlighted the intolerance of "liberals" towards differing views on college campuses and more broadly, arguing that, "liberals think they are tolerant but often they aren't." The CNN host lamented what he called "the campus thought police" who have either uninvited or "booed, interrupted and intimidated" conservative voices such as Heather McDonald and Charles Murray as well as "firebrands" such as Milo Yiannopoulos and Ann Coulter. "It's strange that this is happening on college campuses that promise to give their undergraduates a liberal education," Zakaria said. He attributed this trend to "an attitude of self-righteousness that says we are so pure, we're so morally superior, we cannot bear to hear an idea with which we disagree." While Zakaria is correct to draw attention to this worrying trend, he wrongly conflates liberals and radicals. True liberals encourage dissent, but radicals only support their own right to protest. Bernie Sanders, for example, focuses only on conservative intolerance without criticizing his hard left ideological soul mates for their intolerance. He has characterized The Republican party as "really right-wing extremist," but has not condemned – in fact he has offered his endorsement of – individuals on the hard-left such as Keith Ellison and Jeremy Corbyn, both of whom have histories of intolerance and bigotry against Jews.

This hardening of positions on both sides has been manifested by increasing demands to criminalize political differences. Both sides now scream "lock em up," instead of making substantive criticisms of opposing views.

Never in our history has a presidential administration had calls for impeachment, investigation and indictment begin so early. Indeed, some such calls began even before President Trump was inaugurated. The same was true of Republicans who demanded Hillary Clinton's imprisonment and impeachment even before the election. The fury against Trump is matched only by the fervor in his favor. There were similar, but not nearly as extreme, reactions to the election of President Obama, and I have little doubt, that there would have been renewed calls for Hillary Clinton's prosecution and impeachment had she been elected. Never in recent history has the divisiveness been so extreme. Whatever the reasons – and they include the proliferation of news outlets which create "echo chamber" media, the proliferation of social media, which is susceptible to manipulation, and the global trend away from centrism – the result is a growing extremism that brooks no dissent.

The extensive media focus on whether Trump has committed criminal and/or impeachable offences has had at least one unintended benefit: it has gotten Americans – including young people – to think about our legal and constitutional systems. I recall a teenager asking me to explain what an "emolument" is and why it is prohibited. She said, "before Trump, I though an emolument was a facial cream."[2]

There have been far too few nuanced calls for de-escalation of the mutual demands for criminal prosecution and/ or impeachment. New York Times columnist, David Brooks, has been among the most sober voices. Acknowledging that there is little, if any, evidence that crimes have been committed by Trump or those in his administration, Brooks warns of the perils of "the politics of scandal." He argues: "in the politics of scandal, at least since Watergate, you don't have to engage in persuasion or even talk about issues. Political victories are won when you destroy your political opponents by catching them in some wrongdoing. You get seduced by the delightful possibility that your opponent will be eliminated. Politics is simply about moral superiority and personal

---

2   The Emoluments Clause in Article 1 of the Constitution states: "No Title of Nobility shall be granted by the United States: And no Person holding any Office of Profit or Trust under them, shall, without the Consent of the Congress, accept of any present, Emolument, Office, or Title, of any kind whatever, from any King, Prince, or foreign State." Essentially, the Emoluments Clause prohibits government officials from accepting payments and/or gifts from foreign governments in order to prevent improper external influences. Literally read, it would have precluded President Obama from accepting more than a million dollars from the King of Norway when he won the Nobel Peace Prize early in his presidency. According to sources close to the Nobel Committee, he was given the prize in order to encourage him to promote nuclear disarmament. Congress and accepted practices have created many exceptions to the emoluments clause, including prizes and other honors. It is unlikely that the courts will interpret the clause to cover arms-length business dealings, unless they are so one-sided as to constitute "present[s]."

destruction…the politics is great for those forces responsible for the lawyerization of American life. It takes power out of the hands of voters and elected officials and puts power in the hands of prosecutors and defense attorneys." This transformation of politics into a zero-sum blood sport, in which elections can be undone by prosecution, endangers not only civil liberties, but democracy itself.

MY ROLE

I have staked out a different position from the partisans on both sides. I see my role as defending civil liberties as I have done throughout my life. This is the way I put it to FOX News' Tucker Carlson: "My principles will lead me to conclusions that help one side rather than the other. But I'm not doing it in order to help the Republicans by any means, or [to help] the Democrats. I'm doing it because I care deeply about the constitution and preserving a document that has served us well for over 225 years." This means that I will take positions that sometimes seem to support the Trump administration and sometimes undercut it. Politically, I am a liberal democrat who enthusiastically supported Hillary Clinton and unenthusiastically supported the reelection of Barack Obama (because of his weak foreign policy). But as a civil libertarian, I do not allow the thumb of politics to weight on the scales of justice. I call 'em as I see 'em from a civil liberties perspective without regard to the political implications of my positions.

My role as a civil libertarian has caused many observers to misunderstand my position, or to misstate it when they do understand it. Many people erroneously see me as a political supporter of Donald Trump, rather than a supporter of civil liberties. Some see me as a traitor to the Democratic Party, to liberalism and even to my Jewish heritage. My emails, some of which I quote later, attest to these misunderstandings and distortions. They are also a symptom of the deeper problem: in an age of hyper partisan politics, there is little patience for the non-partisan views of principled civil libertarians. Although I am doing nothing different from what I have done for half a century – defending the civil liberties of those with whom I disagree – my critics sometimes accuse me of having "changed," because they don't like the fact that my current defense of civil liberties helps a president they despise. Not everyone misunderstands me. Some deliberately distort my views.

I have not changed. The civil liberties positions I am now taking with regard to President Trump are the same as those I have taken with regard to politicians of both parties throughout my career. On the eve of the election, when it appeared that Hillary Clinton would win, this is what I wrote: "this election has exacerbated the long-standing problem of criminalizing policy differences. We are quick to confuse differences in policy with charges of criminal behavior. During this election both sides accused the other of criminal conduct... the criminal law must be reserved for willful, deliberate and clearly defined crimes. We are moving away from that understanding and toward a dangerous expansion of the concept of crime in the context of political differences." I also criticized FBI Director Comey for his role in disclosing the email investigation of Hillary Clinton: "the problem revealed by FBI director Comey's ill-advised statements over the past four months will not end with the election...the problem of unlawful FBI leaks has become pervasive. It must be addressed by the new administration." I continued to argue that, "replacing Comey will not be enough, the entire culture of the FBI must be changed and it must be restored to its rightful position as the silent investigative arm of the Justice Department. Indeed, even more fundamental structural changes are now required. The entire Justice Department, of which the FBI is one component, has become too politicized."

Despite my long non-political history of demanding the depoliticization of criminal justice and the de-criminalization of political disagreements, I am attacked by each side when my civil liberties position is seen as supporting their opponents. So be it. At a time when civil liberties have become one of the first casualties of hyper-partisanship, and when the ACLU has succumbed to this malady[3], I see little choice but to stand by my principles, as I did when President Clinton was unfairly subjected to a violation of his civil liberties, as well as when President Nixon was unfairly named as an unindicted co-conspirator, thus denying him the opportunity to defend himself in court. Being a principled civil libertarian is like being a criminal defense lawyer: people love you when you defend their friends and hate you when you defend their enemies. Most Americans like most people in the world, believe in free speech for me but not for thee, due process for political allies but not for enemies,

---

3   See Chapter 4.

objectivity about one's cause but not about other people's causes, especially when they conflict with one's own. Few live by Voltaire's reputed dictum: "I disapprove of what you say, but will defend to the death your right to say it," or to paraphrase it in the current context, "I disagree with your politics and your actions, but will defend your right to due process, fairness and civil liberties."

The *Boston Globe*, in a front-page article entitled "Is Alan Dershowitz defending Trump? Not quite, he says," got it mostly right: "a close reading of Dershowitz's various comments in print and on television suggest he's mostly pushing back against the notion that what Trump is accused of doing amounts to criminal activity. He's not saying what Trump is accused of doing isn't wrong; he's saying it doesn't necessarily appear to be illegal. When asked in a recent television interview whether Trump was indeed the subject of history's greatest political witch hunt, he scoffed and rated it a 4 on a 1-to-10 scale of witch hunts."[4]

A few days before Comey appeared for a hearing before the Senate Intelligence Committee (the first time since he was fired), the Director of Media Affairs at the RNC wrote me a personal email saying: "We are starting to prepare for the response to the Comey hearing on Thursday and wanted to see if you are interested in doing any media. We are happy to facilitate interviews and will provide talking points."

This was my response:

"I'm a liberal Democrat and have no interest in mouthing Republican 'talking points.' The way the RNC went after Hillary Clinton makes it clear you have no interest in civil liberties except as a tactic to defend your party and attack your opponents. Perhaps if you were to defend the civil liberties of people you disagree with – as I do – you could provide me some relevant talking points."

Commitment to civil liberties is an endangered species, as the American left moves closer to the intolerant hard left and as the American right moves closer to the authoritarian hard right. The vibrant center is weakening traditional liberalism and conservatism and diminishing their influence on American political life. Civil liberties have become a tactic to be used selectively in support of ideological causes. I refuse

---

4   https://www.bostonglobe.com/metro/2017/05/24/dershowitz-defending-donald-trump-not-quite-says/JXhTmSoeUdtxWtuxClNiNL/amp.html

to give up on neutral civil liberties and will continue to speak up for them during the Trump administration, even if the result is favorable to a candidate against whom I voted. If evidence of actual crimes were to emerge, I would assess it fairly and report my conclusions honestly, regardless of the impact. And I believe my conclusions would be more credible than those of the pundits and academics who have been "crying wolf"—or in this case screaming "crime"—every time anyone in the Trump administration does something with which they disagree.

This short book will document my approach to these issues in roughly chronological order, beginning with the presidential campaign and continuing through the transition and the first several months of the controversial Trump presidency. It is a work in progress, as is the Trump administration itself, and the investigations being conducted by the special counsel and congressional committees.

We live in "interesting times" – even more interesting since the election of Donald Trump as president. Whether this turns out to be a curse or a blessing may depend on whether we can move away from extremism and closer to the center, bridge our differences, and substitute rational discussion for polemical demands for criminalization of political differences. The objective of this book is to contribute to these important goals, while seeking to preserve the civil liberties of all Americans.

CHAPTER 1

THE RUN UP TO THE CAMPAIGN: BERNIE SANDERS V HILLARY CLINTON

April 26, 2016
HILLARY CLINTON SHOULDN'T MOVE TO THE LEFT

BERNIE SANDERS may no longer be a serious threat to Hillary Clinton's nomination bid, but he and his supporters could still wreak havoc on the Democratic Party this fall. Had Sanders won the nomination, he would likely have been demolished in the general election, as were liberals Michael Dukakis and George McGovern. The difference is Sanders is much further from the party's center than those two candidates were. Sanders' far-left followers would have been marginalized because the Democrats can win only as centrist liberals, not as far-left radicals. But now that Sanders appears to have lost the nomination, his power and that of his supporters, will likely increase — Clinton needs people who "feel the Bern" to sign on to her cause. That will empower not only the real progressives who have been supporting Sanders, but also the repressives who falsely hide their true anti-liberal views under the ill-fitting cloak of progressivism. These repressives have little tolerance for differing viewpoints and seek to shut down speakers who refuse to toe their politically correct line.

Clinton would be smart to resist the temptation to move to the left once she has secured the Democratic nomination. Despite her refusal to use the label "liberal," that's in fact what she is: a centrist liberal who rejects revolution and the radical dismantling of imperfect institutions, such as Obamacare. Like her husband, she should stay in the liberal center, both on domestic and foreign policy issues. That has always been the winning strategy for Democrats, and the Sanders' brush-fire should not change that successful approach.

If Clinton feels the need to move to the far left, she may succeed in the short run in keeping some Sanders' supporters from staying home on Election Day, but she will risk alienating centrist, independent, and undecided voters, who determine the outcome of most national elections. In any event, it is likely that most Sanders' supporters will come out and vote for Clinton, though some who want to shake up the system may support Trump. Far-left zealots, who hate liberals even more than they hate conservatives, may stay home, but their numbers are relatively small, despite the loud noises they emit. Moreover, there is nothing Clinton could do to satisfy the far-left repressives who want to overthrow existing institutions and suppress speech they deem incorrect. These intolerant extremists reject the "politics of respectability" that demands that respect be accorded even to those with whom they disagree.

It is important to understand that the differences between Clinton and far-left Sanderite repressives are not merely matters of degree on many important issues. They are matters of kind. Clinton wants realistic improvements in existing institutions, such as health care, capital markets, banking, the military, our education system, and other structures. Sanders and his far-left followers want revolutionary dismantling of these and other existing institutions. His most radical supporters want even more revolutionary structural changes that would destabilize and weaken our nation. It's not that Sanders is an idealist whose ideas are good but unrealistic, and Clinton a pragmatist whose ideas are compromised with Sanders' ideals. Clinton is right and Sanders is wrong on many key issues over which they disagree. And Clinton should stick to her guns.

Mainstream American voters want evolution, not revolution. They want stability, predictability, and gradual improvements. They don't want to see the United States emulate Europe, where the political pendulum often swings widely between the left and the right and where extremist parties of both the far left and far right are growing in influence. They prefer narrower pendulum swings of the kind seen when first President Clinton (my electoral hope is showing) replaced the first President Bush.

Democracy thrives at the center and suffers when extremists are not marginalized. History has shown that nations caught between the brown of far-right extremism and the red of far-left extremism often choose poorly and suffer grave consequences. Moreover, our system of checks and balances and tripartite division of powers works best when both parties move away from extremes and closer to the center.

Although today's voters are no more extreme than voters in the past, our primary system rewards both Democratic and Republican extremists. The general election, on the other hand, rewards centrists who promise improvement and stability.

Sanders' victories in several state primaries and caucuses may put pressure on Clinton to select as her running mate someone to her left whose views are close to those of Sanders and his base. That would be a serious mistake. In the general election, her Republican opponent will attack her for being too far left, too liberal. If that attack resonates with independents, union members, and undecided voters, she could lose. Clinton's vice presidential choice should be a solid, centrist, trusted figure who comes from a swing state and can appeal to ethnic minorities.

In other words, she should pick the kind of person she would have picked, and campaign for the policies she would have advocated, had Bernie Sanders never entered the race.

June 5, 2016
SANDERS' BIGOTED APPOINTEES ENDANGER CLINTON'S ELECTION

For many years now, support for Israel has been a rare point of bipartisan consensus in an increasingly polarized political climate. Bernie Sanders apparently seems determined to undermine that consensus.

Sanders has demonstrated a consistent bias against the nation-state of the Jewish people and surrounded himself with foreign-policy "experts" who often describe Israel as an apartheid state, and have repeatedly accused the IDF of committing war crimes. Sanders has clearly absorbed some of this rhetoric, as demonstrated in a series of recent interviews, in which he grossly overstated the number of Palestinian civilian deaths in Operation Protective Edge, and accused Israel of using disproportionate force in response to Hamas' rocket attacks.

Here's what he said:

"Sanders: Help me out here, because I don't remember the figures, but my recollection is over 10,000 innocent people were killed in Gaza. Does that sound right?

Daily News: I think it's probably high, but we can look at that.

Sanders: I don't have it in my number... but I think it's over 10,000. My understanding is that a whole lot of apartment houses were leveled. Hospitals, I think, were bombed. So yeah, I do believe and I don't think I'm alone in believing that Israel's force was more indiscriminate than it should have been."

Even the United Nations – whose bias against Israel is well documented – put the number of civilians killed during Operation Protective Edge at 1462, while the Israeli Defense Forces counted 761.

Mr. Sanders' campaign has since attempted to clarify his remarks by claiming that the media distorted Mr. Sanders' comments, and that he was in fact referring to the total number of casualties sustained by the Palestinians over the course of the conflict.

Regardless of whether Mr. Sanders was referring to total casualties or to the death toll, he should apologize for propagating this blatant mistruth. His comments seemed to confirm the wild delusions of anti-Israel zealots, who often seek to delegitimize the nation-state of the Jewish people by accusing its military of deliberately murdering large numbers of innocent Palestinians.

While the media has focused on Bernie Sanders' egregious overstatement of the specific number of innocent Palestinians killed in Operation Protective Edge, the more revealing aspect of what he told the Daily News is his generalization that Israel indiscriminately leveled hospitals and apartment buildings. Although he did not explicitly say that the Israel Defense Forces deliberately targeted civilians and civilian structures, his canard can certainly be understood that way by those Israel haters who are actively supporting his campaign.

The word "indiscriminate," especially applied to Israeli military actions, has acted as a code word among Israel-bashers for war crimes and even genocide. The reality is that the Israeli military efforts to stop Hamas from indiscriminately killing Israeli citizens with rockets and through terror tunnels has been the opposite of indiscriminate. No other country in history has gone to such lengths in trying to distinguish between military and civilian targets, even in the face of an enemy that regularly uses its own population as human shields, and that hides military equipment in schools and hospitals. Israel's efforts to protect its citizens compare favorably to the U.S. and NATO led military bombing campaigns in Iraq, Syria, and other areas, in which civilians have also been used as human shields.

At best, Mr. Sanders' comments on Operation Protective Edge reflect a disappointing lack of interest in the specifics of what happened during the course of the seven-week war. As has been noted by several commentators, Senator Sanders is a long-term elected official who deals with some frequency with the Israeli-Palestinian conflict, and who should be expected to avoid gross misstatements on the topic. Mr. Sanders has done nothing to assuage these concerns: in two recent interviews, Mr. Sanders mistakenly put the number of civilians killed at "over 2,000" and again described the Israeli response as "disproportionate."

Following these statements, primary voters in New York and across the Northeast decisively rejected Sanders' candidacy, and effectively ensured that Hillary Clinton will be the next Democratic presidential nominee. But Sanders' efforts to end the Democratic Party's support for Israel may well endanger Clinton's prospects in the general election.

Rather than modify or moderate his positions on Israel, Sanders now seems intent on remolding the Democratic Party to reflect the views of his most radical anti-Israel (and anti-American) supporters. Sanders apparently wants to use his newfound political clout to revise the language of the Democratic Party platform as regards the only true democracy in the Middle East.

Sanders of course is not alone in accusing Israel of using disproportionate force, but he is very bad company when he cites the "countries all over the world" that have directed this chorus of criticism against Israel. Those who most consistently attack the conduct of the Israeli Defense Forces are among the worst human rights violators in the world, including countries like Saudi Arabia, Iran and Syria.

The reality is that Israel has done what other Western democracies—faced with far less direct threats to their civilians—have done, but they have done so far more carefully, with greater concern for civilians, and to better success. Yet Israel is singled out for unique condemnation as part of a widespread effort to delegitimize, and demonize the nation state of the Jewish people. Sanders has now made statements that lend support to these biased efforts

Reasonable people can disagree with Israel's occupation and settlement policies—although even critics must acknowledge that Israel offered to end the West Bank occupation and settlements in 2000, 2001, and 2008 as part of a plan to create a two-state solution. The Palestinian leadership rejected the 2000 and 2001 offers and failed to respond to the 2008 proposal. Israel did unilaterally end its Gaza occupation and settlements, only to see that area turned into a launching pad for Hamas rockets and tunnels designed to kill Israeli civilians.

Nonetheless, pro-Israel critics, both within and outside of Israel, criticize the current government for not doing more to move toward a two state solution. Whether one agrees or disagrees with this criticism, one can level it without being deemed anti-Israel. But anyone who seeks the mantle of "pro-Israel" has no right to sit in judgment over Israel's military tactics in responding to rocket and tunnel attacks from Gaza. This is especially so if they are as uninformed as Sanders is about the situation on the ground in Israeli cities and town that are close to Gaza. As Barack Obama said when he was running for president and visited Israeli areas that were most directly impacted by rocket attacks: "If somebody was sending rockets into my house where my two daughters sleep at night, I'm going to do everything in my power to stop that. And I would expect Israelis to do the same thing."

Israel has now located and neutralized yet another terror tunnel leading from Gaza into Israel that had been built recently, and already extended "tens of meters" underneath the border fence and into Israel proper. Its purpose is to kill, kidnap and hold hostage Israeli civilians, including children from those towns located near the tunnel exits. The entrances to these deadly military targets have been deliberately placed by Hamas in densely populated areas, rather than in the many sparely populated parts of the Gaza Strip. (Yes there are many such sparsely populated areas, despite the media's demonstrably false claim that the Gaza Strip is among the most densely populated areas of the world. It is less densely populated then Tel Aviv.)

Hamas knows that if they were to deploy their rockets and place the entrances to their terror tunnels in unpopulated areas – as the laws of war require – the Israeli military could attack these military targets without endangering civilians. But Hamas wants Israel to injure and kill its civilians. They deliberately employ what has come to be known by the cruel but accurate term, "the dead baby strategy." Under this double war crime strategy, the Israeli military is put to the terrible Hobson's choice of either allowing its own civilians to be subjected to rocket and tunnel attacks or to destroy those rockets and tunnels by attacking targets that are surrounded by Palestinian civilians, who Hamas effectively uses as human shields.

What would Sanders do if the United State were faced with a comparable dilemma? Would he allow rockets to rain down on American civilians? Would he allow for terror tunnels to ferret armed terrorists to kill and kidnap American children? Or would he do what President Obama urged Israel to do: whatever it takes to stop the rockets and tunnels.

American voters are entitled to know what Sanders would do and what he thinks Israel should do. Would he apply a double standard to the nation state of the Jewish People? Or would he deny the American military the authority to do whatever it takes to protect our citizens? Does he condemn the United States military for using comparable tactics in Afghanistan, Iraq, and Syria? In other words, does Bernie Sanders only believe that Israel has acted disproportionately, or does he also believe that the United States military acts disproportionately? We are entitled to know the answers to these questions, and Bernie Sanders is not entitled to pretend that he is pro-Israel.

Sanders claims that he wants Democrats to embrace a more "balanced approach" to the Israeli-Palestinian conflict, but his appointment of James Zogby and Cornel West to the Democratic Platform Committee suggests anything but. Indeed, both Zogby and West are notorious for espousing policy positions that are extremely critical of Israel, and for using rhetoric that sometimes borders on anti-Semitic.

Zogby, for example, has frequently used provocative and even bigoted language when commentating on the Israeli-Palestinian conflict. He has compared the plight of the Palestinian people to that of the Jews during the Holocaust. He has described Gaza as "the world's largest concentration camp," and has repeatedly accused the Israeli government of perpetrating crimes against humanity. Comparing Israel's self-defense actions to the Nazi genocide against the Jews is a not-so subtle form of Holocaust denial: if all Nazi Germany did was defend itself against Jewish aggression, then there were no gas chambers, no rounding up of Jews from the most far-flung corners of Europe and transporting them to Auschwitz, and no genocide.

Moreover, Zogby has endorsed the Boycott, Divestment and Sanctions movement, which calls for the boycott only of Israeli goods and institutions, until Israel allows for the so-called "right of return," which would turn Israel into yet another Arab-Muslim majority state. In effect Zogby is supportive of a group whose stated objective is to undo over 30 years of negotiations, and end the existence of Israel as the nation state of the Jewish people.

Zogby, however, seems like a moderate in comparison to West, whose frequent diatribes against Israel at times speaks to a propensity for borderline anti-Semitic stereotypes. According to West, for example, the Iraq War was caused by "the close relationship between American imperial elites and Israeli political officials." He has repeatedly accused Israel of killing Palestinian babies – an allegation that echoes historic attacks on Jews for "blood libel" – and frequently claims that Israel is deliberately seeking to annihilate the Palestinian people.

Like many hard-left anti-Israel bigots, West also has disdain for America and its current president, whom he has accused of being a war criminal for supporting Israel's military interventions in Gaza, and for escalating the use of drones in operations against Islamic State (ISIS) and al-Qaida.

He has also called President Barack Obama "the first niggerized president of the United States," a remark which was widely condemned by Republicans and Democrats alike. West justified his criticisms of President Obama by explaining that the president "feels most comfortable with upper middle-class white and Jewish men who consider themselves very smart, very savvy, and very effective in getting what they want" thereby invoking another anti-Semitic stereotype, that of the savvy Jewish businessman.

West has a long history of accusing Jews of being racist. He claimed that "large numbers of Jews tried to secure a foothold in America by falling in step with the widespread perpetuation of anti-black stereotypes and garnering of white-skin privilege benefits to non-black Americans."

Yet it is West who is doing the stereotyping: when West angrily left Harvard for Princeton in 2002 because of a feud with Harvard's then-president Larry Summers, he said that Summers had "messed with the wrong Negro" and called Harvard's Jewish president "the Ariel Sharon of higher education." West also called Black Lives Matter a "marvelous new militancy...with courage, vision," and believes that the shooting of Michael Brown was a manifestation of "American terrorism." West also does not shy away from associating himself with 9/11 conspiracy theorists, going even himself so far as to suggest that one cannot be certain whether Muslims were behind the attacks.

Sanders' decision to elevate radicals like West and Zogby to positions of power within the Democratic Party speaks to either a stunning lack of judgment or an underlying hostility toward the nation-state of the Jewish people. Either way, it must be resisted by the much-maligned Democratic Party establishment come the convention in July.

Hillary Clinton has already made significant concessions to the so-called progressive wing of the party represented by Sanders. On issues like free trade, the minimum wage and regulation of the financial industry she has moved toward Sanders in meaningful ways. As far as Israel is concerned, however, Clinton must stand her ground and oppose the fringe positions of the far-left. If she does not, she may well suffer among centrist voters in several swing states.

Sanders seems determined to turn Israel into a partisan issue by appointing surrogates like Zogby and West to rewrite the Democratic Party platform.

It is up to centrist Democrats, who still represent a majority of the party, to resist this attempt, and to ensure that support for Israel remains a point of bipartisan consensus. Weakening this historic consensus would be bad for Israel, for America, for peace – and for the electoral prospects of the Democratic Party.

June 27, 2016
POST-BREXIT, US NEEDS A CENTRIST LEADER

The United Kingdom has long been a paragon of cautious political centrism. For the past several decades, British prime ministers — Conservative and Labour alike — have governed from the center to great effect, with considerable stability, both political and financial. That stability may now be ending with last week's vote to leave the European Union.

First and foremost, Brexit is a rejection of the centrist political consensus and a victory for the extreme populism embodied by Nigel Farage, the leader of the far-right UKIP party. For the rest of Europe, Brexit continues a worrying trend, which has seen the empowerment of populist parties, at the expense of the moderate, technocratic status quo. Hungary, Poland, and Slovakia have all elected far-right governments whose nationalistic rhetoric and censorship of dissent echo an earlier, darker period of European history. In France, the National Front, which only a decade ago was led by a rabid anti-Semite, made significant inroads in France's recent presidential election. In Spain, the far-left party, Podemos, is now the second largest political alignment in the country, and in Italy, polls show that the self-described populist Five Star Movement has become the country's most popular political party.

Time and again, history has demonstrated that extremism in politics, whether right or left, is dangerous to the world. Today, voters in Europe seem intent on forgetting that lesson. Slowly but surely, European centrist liberalism is dying, along with centrist conservatism. Indeed, the increasing influence of the hard right has served to increase the influence of the hard left and vice versa. Both weaken the center and move the world away from stability, rationality, tolerance, and nuance — and toward demagoguery, simple mindedness, xenophobia and intolerance.

At best, this polarized political climate encourages the formation of self-contained opinion echo chambers. At worst, it leads to violence, as we saw with the murder of a pro-EU member of Parliament, Jo Cox, by a suspect who reportedly shouted "Britain first" as he pulled out his weapon.

Following the British vote to leave the European Union, former prime minister Tony Blair warned of what could happen to Europe if the center does not hold: " If we do not succeed in beating back the far left and far right before they take the nations of Europe on this reckless experiment, it will end the way such rash action always does in history: at best, in disillusion; at worst, in rancorous division. The center must hold."

It could happen in the United States as well, if the center fails to hold.

The Republicans have nominated a candidate who has vowed to drain the swamp of politics as usual and shake up the established center. Republican primary and caucus voters rejected centrist candidates such as Jeb Bush, John Kasich, and Marco Rubio.

Democratic voters cast millions of ballots for a populist candidate from the extreme left whose supporters included advocates of violence, revolution, and civil disobedience.

Fortunately for the Democrats, America, and the world, a reasonable, centrist, responsible presidential candidate has emerged. The election of Hilary Clinton is now imperative, not only for the stability of our nation but also for the stability of the world.

The election of Clinton will help achieve such stability at a dangerous time. And in order to win, she must present herself as a stabilizing centrist. To do that, she must select a vice presidential candidate who is also a centrist rather than a Sanderista.

A world with wide pendulum swings between the hard right and the hard left is a dangerous place. Clinton, should campaign, win, and govern from the center. This will not be easy. Centrism has become synonymous with a boring and dysfunctional political status quo, and there is great temptation — especially at a time of increasing popular unrest — to pander to the extremes embodied by the "movement" politics that define the Donald Trump and Bernie Sanders candidacies. But this temptation must be resisted in the name of much-needed stability. The stakes are now higher than the future of the United States. What is at stake in this election is the future stability of the world.

CHAPTER 2
THE CAMPAIGN: DONALD TRUMP VS. HILLARY CLINTON

June 9, 2016
ADVICE TO CLINTON: DON'T TRY TO PLACATE SANDERS'S HARD-LEFT VOTERS

Even following Hillary Clinton's historic victory in the primaries, there are some among the most radical Bernie Sanders supporters – let's call them Sanderistas – who would actually like to see Donald Trump beat Hillary Clinton in the general election. Their "logic" is as follows: If Clinton wins, Sanders becomes just another loser. The Sanderistas become marginalized. And their leader's quest for a political revolution ends with the election of yet another centrist "establishment" Democrat.

However, if Trump beats Clinton, Sanders will claim to become the titular leader of the Democratic Party, pointing to early polls showing that he would have beaten Trump, though these polls signify little about how he would have done in an actual head-to-head contest. (In my opinion, he would have suffered a devastating defeat comparable to those suffered by other left-wing candidates such as Walter Mondale (1984) and Michael Dukakis (1988), though nothing is predictable with Trump as the Republican nominee.) Moreover, were Clinton to lose, Sanders's influence would increase within the party – and around the country – because the Sanderistas would take credit for Clinton's defeat and insist that without them the Democrats can't win a general election.

Other Sanderistas have put forward a more destructive rationale. As one of Sanders's most prominent surrogates, the actress Susan Sarandon explained, "[S]ome people feel that Donald Trump will bring the revolution immediately if he gets in, things will really explode."

Sarandon, who made the same case for Ralph Nader in the 2000 presidential election (and look how that turned out), is not the only Sanders supporter who feels that a Trump presidency could be the catalyst for the leftist political revolution promised by Sanders and his surrogates.

These hard-left radicals, just like their anti-establishment counterparts on the extreme Right, believe that the nomination system is rigged if they do not get their way.

Ultimately, it's unsurprising that Trump has seized on that sentiment and invited them to join forces in the quest for a revolution: "To all of those Bernie Sanders voters who have been left out in the cold by a rigged system of superdelegates, we welcome you with open arms."

As she struggles to unify the Democratic Party, however, Clinton should be wary: Any effort to embrace the Sanderistas will backfire.

They won't vote for her anyway, unless she goes so far Left as to fall off the political cliff. As CNN recently reported, "Sanders has inspired a movement, but it's unclear whether he can control it. Or if he wants to... [M]any [of his supporters] insist they will not fall into line behind Hillary Clinton... They are taking seriously Sanders's call for a political revolution, complicating any hope for quick unity with Clinton."

One such Sanderista is quoted as saying, "You can't expose the corruption of the political system and then expect us to get behind that same political system." Another threatens that "[i]f Bernie Sanders does not walk out of that thing as the nominee, we can guarantee you from that point on we'll start the de-registration of the Democratic Party. They have a choice to make."

Even if some Sanderistas were to rally to Clinton, their votes in swing states would not be enough to have a meaningful impact on the general election, especially in comparison to the support she would lose in the political Center, which has little appetite for revolution. Moreover, any appeasement of the far Left will be welcomed by the Republican Party, which now fears that its centrist wing will defect in large numbers, and vote for Clinton, because its members view Trump with disdain. If Clinton embraces the Sanderistas, these voters will view the election as a contest between the kooky Right and the equally kooky Left. Given that choice, they will prefer their right-wing kook to the leftwing kook.

This is not to say that Clinton should not consider supporting reasonable programs just because they were advocated by Sanders.

She already has, and should continue, talked about reducing the gap between the rich and the poor, raising the minimum wage, rethinking trade agreements, holding Wall Street accountable, making college more affordable and other domestic economic fixes.

She staked out that territory in her speeches and she should continue to try to appeal to reasonable Sanders voters, especially among the young.

However, there are two particular areas where the Sanders program would endanger Clinton's electoral prospects. The first is domestic: She should not adopt Sanders economics of spending more than a reasonable budget would permit. Adopting pie in the sky proposals that would add trillions of dollars to the budget and dramatically increase the national debt would be a gift to Trump. Americans don't want to be debtors who mortgage their children's future. We want reasonable spending that we can afford.

The second gift to Trump would be in the area of foreign policy, particularly with regard to the Middle East. Were Clinton to move away from support for Israel, it could hurt her electoral chances in several swing states.

Americans in general admire and support Israel.

The don't want a president who would parrot the views of radical Israel-haters such as Cornel West and James Zogby who falsely accuse Israel of being an apartheid state that sets up concentration camps and aims to annihilate Palestinians. Even many of Sanders's young supporters, some of whom are critical of certain Israeli policies, especially with regard to the settlements, do not want the US to adopt the West-Zogby anti-Israel approach.

Sanders received his support from young people for his domestic policy, not his foreign policy (about which he knows little). He wandered into the morass of Mideast politics only to satisfy his hard-left supporters who think in absurd packages: If you support the environment and higher minimum wages, then you must oppose Israel. That's not the way centrist and independent voters think, and Clinton must reject that kind of radical "intersectional" thinking if she is to beat Trump in the fall.

So let Hillary be Hillary and not become Bernie.

Let her look for guidance to the successful centrist politics of Barack Obama and Bill Clinton, rather than the failed revolutionary screeds of Bernie Sanders, Cornel West and Susan Sarandon. We are a centrist nation that has thrived without the turmoil that extremes – both left and right – bring to politics and governance. We don't want to emulate

Europe and South America, which often alternate between socialist and nationalist regimes – between the Red and the Brown. If she gets too close to the hard-left politics of Sanders' most extreme "Bernie or bust" zealots, she may get burned in the general election – and so will our nation.

July 6, 2016
DID FBI DIRECTOR COMEY EXCEED HIS AUTHORITY?

FBI Director James Comey's statement recommending against prosecuting Hillary Clinton was unusual in several respects. First, it is not generally regarded as the job of the FBI to make judgment calls about whether or not to prosecute. Those judgment calls are supposed to be made by prosecutors. The job of the FBI is to investigate the facts and lay them out as objectively and completely as possible so that prosecutors can exercise their discretion and judgment.

Although technically the attorney general in this case could exercise independent judgment, she is unlikely to do so, having already said she would defer to the FBI's recommendation. So in this instance the FBI found the facts, applied the law and exercised prosecutorial discretion. A strange role for an investigative agency!

Second, it is unusual for an FBI director to express opinions such as the kind that Comey made in his statement. He said that Clinton had been "extremely careless" in her handling of sensitive material. That is not a legal concept, but to lay people it could sound very much like "gross negligence," which is one of the statutory criteria for bringing a prosecution.

Normally when a prosecutor declines prosecution, all that is said is that there will be no indictment. It is rare, though not unprecedented, for a prosecutor to then go on to excoriate the object of the investigation. The question should be asked: Is that a proper role for the director of the FBI?

Third, Comey used an unusual verbal formulation in discussing classified information. This is what he said:

"Only a small number of the emails containing classified information bore markings indicating the presence of classified information."

He did not explain what he meant by the words "bore markings." Does this mean that they were stamped "classified"? Or does it mean that there were indications within the text of the emails that would show that it was in fact classified? The confusion was exacerbated by Comey's next sentence in which he said the following:

"But even if information is not marked 'classified' in an email, participants who know or should know that the subject is classified are obligated to protect it."

Comey's use of the words "marked classified" seems to suggest that there is a distinction between emails that were marked "classified" and emails that "bore markings indicating the presence of classified information."

This use of different verbal formulations suggests that none of the emails were actually marked "classified." I may be wrong in that surmise, but it is certainly suggested by how Comey used these different formulations.

Fourth, Comey went out of his way to say that even if there is no basis for criminal prosecution, there might be other sanctions that could be applied to all those who participated in email exchanges that contained classified material.

This statement suggests that several of Clinton's most important aides may eventually be denied security clearance, which would prevent them from serving in sensitive positions in the government if she were to win. The decision whether to grant or deny security clearance should be made at the relevant time, by the relevant authorities, not by the FBI in anticipation of future possibilities.

Putting aside these unusual aspects of the Comey statement, he was certainly correct in his ultimate recommendation. The evidence in this case, as he described it, would not have justified a criminal prosecution.

There is simply no precedent for indicting a former Secretary of State for carelessness, even extreme carelessness. This is especially true when the former secretary is about to become her party's nominee for president. Directors of the FBI should not be influencing the outcome of presidential elections unless there is a clear and unequivocal violation of the law.

In general, the principal of "lenity" — which requires doubts to be resolved in close cases against prosecution — applies even more strictly when the decision to indict would effectively deny the public the right to exercise its judgment about who should be the president.

So the bottom line is that Clinton will not be indicted, but the director of the FBI has issued a statement that may have a considerable impact on the upcoming election. This raises fundamental structural questions about the role of the FBI in investigating political figures.

We must never forget that the building in which Comey works bears the name of one of his predecessors, J. Edgar Hoover. We must all ask ourselves the question whether we would trust another Hoover to make the kinds of decisions that Comey has made in this case.

If the answer to that question is "no," then we must consider structural changes that would prevent a future J. Edgar Hoover from exercising the kind of power exercised by James Comey in this case.

September 14, 2016
THIS ELECTION IS UNPREDICTABLE

This is the strangest presidential election in my memory. Despite the polls, the outcome is utterly unpredictable. This was true even before Hillary Clinton's recent health issue. Just consider this: it was only a month ago that *The Washington Post* declared a landslide victory for Hillary Clinton.

"[A] dispassionate examination of the data, combined with a coldblooded look at the candidates, the campaigns and presidential elections, produces only one possible conclusion: Hillary Clinton will defeat Donald Trump in November... Three months from now, with the 2016 presidential election in the rearview mirror, we will look back and agree that the presidential election was over on Aug. 9th."

On August 24, *Slate*, a liberal online magazine owned by *The Washington Post*, similarly declared, "There is no horse race: it's Clinton by a mile, with Trump praying for black swans" — only to "predict" one week later "Trump-Clinton Probably Won't be A Landslide." A few days ago, in a desperate attempt to analyze the new polls showing Trump closing in on Clinton, *Slate* explained sheepishly, "Things realistically couldn't have gotten much worse for Trump than they were a few weeks ago, and so it's not a shock that they instead have gotten a little better of late." Some current polls even show Trump with a slight lead.

The reality is that polling is incapable of accurately predicting the outcome of elections like this one, where so many voters are angry, resentful, emotional, negative, and frightened. In my book, *Electile Dysfunction: A Guide for the Unaroused Voter* I discuss in detail why so many voters now say they won't vote at all, or will vote for a third-party candidate. As *The New York Times* reported, "Only 9% of America Chose Trump and Clinton as the Nominees." Or to put the voter's frustration with the candidates more starkly, "Eighty-one percent of Americans say they would feel afraid following the election of one of the two polarizing politicians."

Despite their perceived lack of agency, these voters may, of course, end up voting for one of the two major candidates when Election Day comes around.

This may depend in part on whether the Johnson-Weld ticket does well enough in the polls to be included in the presidential and vice presidential debates. The rules require that a third-party candidate reach 15 percent in five national polls. This number is difficult to achieve because many of the polls do not include third-party candidates. But it is not impossible, and if it were to occur, and if the Johnson-Weld ticket outperformed or held its own against Clinton and Trump, then people who had decided not to vote or who couldn't make up their minds might cast ballots for the Libertarian candidates. [Ultimately, the Johnson-Weld ticket did not qualify for the presidential and vice-presidential debates and the presidential race was largely fought between Trump and Clinton.]

It is unlikely that the Stein/Baraka ticket will be included in the debates or that it will garner any significant number of voters in key states, because the candidates are so extreme in their views and so out of the mainstream of American political beliefs. However, if a significant number of voters do vote for a third or fourth party, this could impact the election, as the votes for Ralph Nader in 2000 may have determined the Florida outcome, which in turn determined the general election outcome.

The bottom line is that in a bizarre election like this one — with so many variables and so much emotion — polls may well under- or over-predict votes for the two major candidates. Think about the vote on Brexit. Virtually all the polls — including exit polls that asked voters what they had voted for — got it wrong. The financial markets got it wrong.

The bookies got it wrong. The 2016 presidential election is more like the Brexit vote in many ways than it is like prior presidential elections. Both Brexit and this presidential election involve raw emotion, populism, anger, nationalism, class division, and other factors that distort accuracy in polling. So anyone who thinks they know who will be the next president of the United States is deceiving themselves!

To be sure, the Electoral College vote is sometimes less difficult to predict than the popular vote, because it generally turns on a handful of closely contested critical states, such as Ohio, Florida, Pennsylvania, and Virginia. But in this election, there could be surprises in states that are usually secure for one party or the other. So even the electoral vote will be more difficult to predict than in previous elections.

One reason for this unique unpredictability is the unique unpredictability of Donald Trump himself. No one really knows what he will say or do between now and the election. His position on important issues may change. Live televised debates will not allow him to rely on a teleprompter, as he largely did in his acceptance speech or in his speech during his visit to Mexico City. He may once again become a loose cannon. No one can predict what he will say or do next. This may gain him votes, or it may lose him votes. Just remember: few, if any, pundits accurately predicted how far Trump would get when he first entered the race. When it comes to Donald Trump, the science of polling seems inadequate to the task.

Hillary Clinton is more predictable, but her past actions may produce unpredictable results, as they did when FBI Director James Comey characterized her conduct with regard to her emails as "extremely careless." It is also possible that more damaging information about her private email server or the Clinton Foundation may come from WikiLeaks or other such sources (whether these "revelations" are actually incriminating seems to be beside the point for those 54% of voters who, without first-hand knowledge of the investigation, suspect that the FBI engaged in a preferential treatment by not seeking criminal charges against Clinton.) Finally, it is difficult to assess what impact, if any, her health issues may have had on voters.

Another unpredictable factor that may impact the election is whether there are terrorist attacks in the lead-up to the voting. Islamic extremists would almost certainly like to see Trump beat Clinton, because they believe a Trump presidency would result in the kind of instability on which they thrive. If ISIS attacks American targets in late October, that could turn some undecided voters in favor of the candidate who says he will do anything to stop terrorism. If voters were to change their votes based on terrorist acts, that would only encourage more terrorism in the run-up to elections.

A final reason why this election is so unpredictable is because voter turnout is unpredictable. The "Bernie or bust" crowd is threatening to stay home or vote for the Green Party. Young voters may do here what they did in Great Britain: many failed to vote in the Brexit referendum and then regretted their inaction when it became clear that if they had voted in the same proportion as older voters, Brexit would likely have been defeated. Some Clinton supporters worry that black voters who voted in large numbers for Barack Obama may cast fewer votes for Clinton in this election. Voters who usually vote Republican but can't bring themselves to pull the lever for Trump may decide to stay home. Turnout is unpredictable, and the effect of low voter turnout is also unpredictable.

So for all these reasons and others, no one can tell how this election will turn out. It would be a real tragedy and an insult to democracy if the election were to be decided by those who fail to vote, rather than by those who come out to vote for or against one of the two major candidates.

October 30, 2016

Comey's Statements on Clinton Emails Raise Disturbing Questions

The recent letters sent by FBI Director James Comey raise important questions to which the voters are entitled to answers.

The first and most important is whether Comey, before he sent his letter, was actually aware of the content of the emails that were found on Anthony Weiner's devices. In his original letter, he informed Congress that, "the FBI has learned of the existence of emails that appear to be pertinent to the investigation."

Subsequent reporting suggests that at the time that he made this statement he was not aware of their content. Indeed, in his original letter, he indicated that, "the FBI should take appropriate investigative steps designed to allow investigators to review these emails…"

In his subsequent letter to FBI employees, he said that the FBI "should take appropriate steps to obtain and review them." This strongly suggests that at the time he wrote these letters, Comey had not himself reviewed the content of the emails nor had he been informed of their content by his investigators.

How then could Comey know that the emails may be "pertinent to the investigation?" The clear implication of Comey's communications, which he knew would be made public, was that a) The emails may contain information "pertinent to the investigation;" b) They were not already turned over to the FBI pursuant to earlier requests; c) They involve Hillary Clinton.

Comey's statements may well impact the result of the election, even if he had no intention of doing so. He may well have made the following calculation: Clinton is so far ahead that she will probably win. If she wins and subsequent investigation produces evidence damning to Clinton, which was not disclosed before the election, he would be faulted by Donald Trump and the Republicans for impacting the election by his silence.

But there is another side to this coin which he should, but may not, have considered: What if his statements about the emails produce a victory for Trump and it then turns out that there was nothing of significance in them? Or that they were merely duplicates of what had already been produced? [This ultimately turned out to be the case and the FBI confirmed that this batch of emails were merely duplicates.]

There was a third alternative that Comey could have employed that would have reduced the possibility of his statements improperly impacting the election.

He could have said the following, with clarity and without ambiguity: "The FBI has just learned that there are emails to and from Huma Abedin on the devices we obtained from Anthony Weiner during the sexting investigation.

Neither I nor my investigators have seen these emails. At this time, we have no idea whether they are duplicates of what has already been produced or whether they contain any information pertinent to the investigation of Hillary Clinton's emails. We simply do not know. Nobody should presume therefore that there is anything pertinent to our investigation, or incriminating, in any of these emails. We won't know that until we have accessed and read these emails and compared them to those previously disclosed.

I feel obligated to tell Congress about this development, but because we are not yet aware of the content of the emails, it would be unfair for any candidate or voter to infer from my letter that there is anything in them relevant to the election. This is especially the case since it is unlikely that our investigation will be completed before the election."

But that is not what Comey said; that is not what the media reported; and that is not how voters perceive the impact of Comey's disclosure.

At this point Comey has only two options if he is to maintain his neutrality in the election. First he must either issue a statement of the kind described above, or second he must undertake a crash investigation and make a further disclosure in the coming days so that voters will know whether there is anything in the emails should properly impact their votes.

Of course, much of the damage may already have been done, since early voting will take place between the time he issued his initial letter and the time he takes the steps outlined above.

Reporting has indicated that none of the newly discovered emails are from Hillary Clinton. It is unlikely, therefore, that these emails contain incriminating information sufficient to result in a criminal prosecution of her.

Nonetheless, these disclosures raise an interesting, if hypothetical, constitutional question: What if Hillary Clinton were elected and then evidence of criminality were revealed. Could she, as president, pardon herself before any investigation was complete? This hypothetical has intrigued law professors and legal scholars since the Watergate scandal involving Richard Nixon, who did not pardon himself, but was pardoned by his successor, Gerald Ford.

The answer to the question of whether a president may pardon him or herself is crystal clear: Nobody knows for sure.

The text of the Constitution grants the president the "power to grant reprieves and pardons for offenses against the United States, except in cases of impeachment." This would seem absolute and not subject to constraints either from Congress, the courts or legal ethics.

Since crimes committed before a president takes office may not be impeachable offenses, the second clause of the constitutional provision would not limit the president. But the common law and long accepted rules of legal ethics preclude anyone from being a judge in his or her own case. A president pardoning herself would be engaging in a massive conflict of interest that the public would never accept, just as it didn't accept Nixon's firing of the special prosecutor Archibald Cox.

Indeed, a self-pardon might well constitute an impeachable offense even if the underlying crime did not fit that category.

I am confident that this dire situation will not arise in our current election. Hillary Clinton will not be indicted in the email investigation. Nor will Donald Trump be indicted for fraud in the Trump University matter. A far graver danger would be if a president were to be elected based on false information or information that was widely misunderstood by voters.

That is why FBI director Comey cannot remain silent following the release of his ill-advised statements. [I was ultimately proved right, and Director Comey was forced to publicly clarify his imprudent statement and the FBI's findings before the election.]

November 1, 2016

OBAMA: DON'T DESTROY THE PEACE PROCESS BY TURNING IT OVER TO THE U.N.

The Obama Administration is sending strong signals that once the election is over it may make a major push to resolve the Israeli-Palestinian conflict at the United Nations

Despite repeated invitations by Israeli Prime Minister Benjamin Netanyahu to Palestinian Authority President Abbas to meet without preconditions, the stalemate persists. Some blame it on Palestinian unwillingness to recognize Israel as the nation state of the Jewish People and to compromise to the so-called "right of return." Others — including the current U.S. Administration — lay the blame largely at the feet of the Netanyahu government for continuing to build in the West Bank, most recently approval of between 98 and 300 new homes in Shiloh. Whatever the reasons – and they are complex and multifaceted — President Obama should resist any temptation, during his final weeks in office, to change longstanding American policy — that only direct negotiations between the parties will achieve a lasting peace.

In particular, Obama should veto an expected French resolution in the Security Council establishing an international peace conference under the auspices of the U.N. The general parameters of the French resolution would likely call for:

"Borders based on the 1967 Lines with agreed equivalent land swaps; security arrangements preserving the sovereignty of the Palestinian State and guaranteeing the security of Israel; a fair, equitable, and negotiated solution to the refugee problem; an arrangement making Jerusalem the capital of both states."

These guidelines may sound reasonable. Indeed, they are strikingly similar to the offers made to and reject by the Palestinian leadership in 2000-2001 from former Israeli Prime Minister Ehud Barak and former U.S. President Bill Clinton, and in 2008 by former Israeli Prime Minister Ehud Olmert. The U.N., however, has disqualified itself from playing any constructive role in the peace process. Recent attempts by the U.N. to intervene in the Israeli-Palestinian conflict have produced unmitigated disasters. The so-called Goldstone Report, which sought to investigate allegations of war crimes committed during the 2009 Israeli intervention in Gaza, was so blatantly biased against Israel that Richard Goldstone himself had to retract some of its key findings in 2011.

Since then, the U.N. has done nothing to reassure Israel that it is capable of offering an unbiased forum for negotiations. In the past year alone, the U.N. has singled out Israel for special criticism on issues like health rights, and most laughably, women's rights, while failing even to mention regimes whose record on these issues is truly abominable. Last year alone, at least twenty separate resolutions were adopted by the U.N. General Assembly, which singled out Israel for special criticism. Most recently UNESCO attempted to erase millennia of Jewish history with regard to the Temple Mount in Jerusalem. In light of such behavior, the U.S. should not trust that Israel would receive a fair hearing at any U.N. sponsored peace conference.

As Netanyahu said in his most recent speech to the U.N. General Assembly, "The road to peace runs through Jerusalem and Ramallah, not through New York." In other words, the only way forward for the Israeli-Palestinian peace process is bilateral negotiations between the two parties. Netanyahu and Abbas must sit down and agree to necessary but painful compromises aimed at establishing a Palestinian state, while addressing Israel's security concerns, and the realities on the ground.

Resolutions such as the proposed French resolution undermine such efforts by encouraging the Palestinians to believe that direct negotiations — and the mutual sacrifices they would entail — are unnecessary, and that a Palestinian state can be achieved on the basis of U.N. resolutions alone. It would also make it more difficult, if not impossible, for the Palestinian Authority to accept anything less than that already given them by the U.N. — which would in turn guarantee the failure of any realistic negotiations.

It is for these and other reasons that American policy has long been to veto or otherwise derail U.N. attempts to interfere with the Israeli-Palestinian peace process even when it is stalled. As President Obama said in 2013:

"We seek an independent, viable and contiguous Palestinian state as the homeland of the Palestinian people. The only way to achieve that goal is through direct negotiations between Israelis and Palestinians themselves."

Hillary Clinton, too, has stated in the past, that she supports bilateral negotiations between the Israelis and Palestinians, and her campaign has said that she "believes that a solution to this conflict cannot be imposed from without." So, too, has Donald Trump.

Recently, however, several past and present Obama officials have apparently advised the president to support, or at least not veto the French resolution, as well as a one-sided Palestinian push to have the U.N. declare Israeli settlements illegal. It would be wrong — and undemocratic — for Obama to unilaterally reverse decades of U.S. foreign policy during the lame duck period. After all, in 2011 his administration vetoed an almost identical Palestinian proposal that called for Israel to "immediately and completely cease all settlement activities in occupied Palestinian territory, including East Jerusalem." Similarly, until now, Obama has repeatedly pressured the French and other European nations not to put forward any proposal related to the Israeli-Palestinian conflict, on the grounds that such initiatives discourage bilateral negotiations. This is surely the view of the majority of the Senate, which has its own constitutional authority to participate in foreign policy decisions. In fact, 88 senators signed an open letter to Obama in which they called on the President to veto any Security Council resolutions regarding the Israeli-Palestinian conflict.

The period between the election and the inauguration is the only time a president can act without the checks and balances of American democracy. He should not take action that would tie the hands of his successor.

Obama must realize that no lasting peace can be achieved in the remaining months of his presidency: there are a multitude of complex and contentious issues — most notably the status of Jerusalem, the rights of so-called Palestinian refugees, and the situation in Gaza — that must be thoroughly addressed in order to achieve a lasting peace. Our next president will undoubtedly have to wade into the Israeli-Palestinian peace process again. The new administration — with the agreement of the Senate — should have full latitude to do what it deems most appropriate. It should not be stuck with parameters bequeathed to it by a President desperate to secure a short-term foreign policy "victory" that in the long term will make a resolution of the conflict more difficult to achieve.

If Obama feels that he must intrude in an effort to break the logjam before he leaves office, he should suggest that the current Israeli government offer proposals similar to those offered in 2000-2001 and 2008 and that this time the Palestinian leadership should accept them in face-to-face negotiations. But he should take no action (or inaction) that invites U.N. involvement in the peace process — involvement that would guarantee failure for any future president's efforts to encourage a negotiated peace.

We should hear the views of both candidates on whether the U.S. should support or veto a Security Council resolution that would tie their hands were they to be elected president. It is not too late to stop President Obama from destroying any realistic prospects for peace.

September 11, 2015
A RIGGED VOTE, NO REAL DEBATE[5]

When I was growing up, "filibuster" was a dirty word. It was a tactic used by bigoted Southern Senators to prevent the enactment of any civil

---

5   The next two columns, which are out of chronological order, demonstrate a pattern during President Obama's second term.

rights legislation. I recall Senator Strom Thurmond babbling on for 24 hours in an effort to keep the South racially segregated. We regarded the filibuster as the enemy of democracy and the weapon of choice against civil rights.

Yet, President Obama and his followers in the senate deployed this undemocratic weapon in order to stifle real debate about the nuclear deal with Iran and to prevent the up or down vote promised by the Corker bill. A President who was more confident of the deal, would have welcomed the Lincoln-Douglas type debates that I and others had called for regarding the most important foreign policy decision of the 21st century. But instead of arguments on the merits and demerits of the deal, what we mostly got was *ad hominems*. Proponents of the deal trotted out famous names of those who supported the deal, without detailed arguments about why they took that position. No wonder so few Americans support the deal. According to a recent Pew poll approximately one in five Americans think the deal is a good one. The President had an obligation to use his bully pulpit to try to obtain majority support among voters. Not only did he fail to do that, he also failed to persuade a majority of senator and house members. So this minority deal will go into operation over the objection of majority of our legislators and voters.

One of the low points of this debate was a variation on the ad hominem fallacy. It was the argument by religious or ethnic identity. Supporters of the deal tried to get as many prominent Jews as they could to sign ads and petitions in favor of the deal. The implicit argument was, "See, even Jews support this deal, so it must be good for Israel," despite the reality that the vast majority of Israelis and almost all of its political leaders believe the deal is bad for Israel.

The absolute low point in the non-debate was a *New York Times* chart, identifying opponents of the deal by whether they were Jewish or Gentile. The implication was that Jews who opposed the deal must be more loyal to their Jewish constituents or to Israel than Americans who supported the deal. But the chart itself made little sense. It turns out that the vast majority of democratic Congressmen who voted against the deal were not Jewish, and several of them represented districts in which less than 1% of the voters were Jewish. It is true that two out of the four democratic senators who voted against the deal were identified as Jews, but one of the non-Jewish Senators represents West Virginia where

Jewish voters constituted less than one tenth of one percent of the voting population. Moreover, opposition to this deal is considerably greater among evangelical Christians than among Jews.

Identifying by their religion members of congress who voted against a deal that the *Times* strongly supported is, as the Committee for Accuracy in Middle East Reporting (CAMERA) aptly put it, more than a dog whistle; it is a bull horn. It plays squarely into anti-Semitic stereotypes of Jews having dual loyalty. Will the *Times* next identify bankers, media moguls, journalists and professors by their religious identity? Would the *Times* have done that for other ethnic, religious or gender groups?

This has been a bad month for democracy, for serious debate and for the treatment of all Americans as equally capable of deciding important issues on their merits and demerits. Whether it also turns out to have been a bad month for peace and nuclear non-proliferation remains to be seen. But even those who support the deal should be ashamed of some of the undemocratic tactics and bigoted arguments employed to avoid a real debate and a majority vote.

April 25, 2016

OBAMA MUST APOLOGIZE FOR DOUBLE STANDARD TOWARD NETANYAHU

As President Obama winds up his farewell tour of Europe, it is appropriate to consider the broader implications of the brouhaha he created in Great Britain. At a joint press conference with Britain Prime Minister, David Cameron, President Obama defended his intrusion into British politics in taking sides on the controversial and divisive Brexit debate. In an op-ed, Obama came down squarely on the side of Britain remaining in the European Union – a decision I tend to agree with on its merits. But he was much criticized by the British media and British politicians for intruding into a debate about the future of Europe and Britain's role in it.

Obama defended his actions by suggesting that in a democracy, friends should be able to speak their minds, even when they are visiting another country: "If one of our best friends is in an organization that enhances their influence and enhances their power and enhances their economy, then I want them to stay in. Or at least I want to be able to tell them 'I think this makes you guys bigger players.'" Nor did he stop at merely giving the British voters unsolicited advice, he also issued a not so veiled threat. He said that "The UK is going to be in the back of the queue" on trade agreements if they exit the EU.

President Obama must either have a short memory or must adhere to Emerson's dictum that "foolish consistency is the hobgoblin of little minds." Recall how outraged the same President Obama was when the Prime Minister of a friendly country, Benjamin Netanyahu, spoke his mind about the Iran Deal.

There are, of course, differences: first, Israel has a far greater stake in the Iran deal than the United States has in whatever decision the British voters make about Brexit: and second, Benjamin Netanyahu was representing the nearly unanimous view of his countrymen, whereas there is little evidence of whether Americans favor or oppose Brexit in large numbers.

Another difference, of course, is that Obama was invited to speak by Cameron, whereas, Netanyahu was essentially disinvited by Obama. But under our tripartite system of government — which is different than Britain's Unitary Parliamentary system — that fact is monumentally irrelevant. Netanyahu was invited by a co-equal branch of the government, namely Congress, which has equal authority over foreign policy with the president and equal authority to invite a friendly leader. Moreover, not only are the British voters divided over Brexit, but the conservative party itself is deeply divided. Indeed, the leading political figure in opposition to Britain remaining in the European Union is a potential successor to Cameron as leader of the Conservative party. So these differences certainly don't explain the inconsistency between Obama's interference in British affairs and his criticism of Netanyahu for accepting an invitation from Congress to express his country's views on an issue directly affecting its national security.

So what is it Mr. President? Should friends speak their minds about controversial issues when visiting another country, or should they keep their views to themselves? Or is your answer that friends should speak their minds only when they agree with other friends, but not when they disagree? Such a view would skew the market place of ideas beyond recognition. If friends should speak about such issues, it is even more important to do so when they disagree.

A wit once observed that "hypocrisy is the homage vice pays to virtue." It is also the currency of diplomacy and politics. That doesn't make it right.

The President owes the American people, and Benjamin Netanyahu, an explanation for his apparent hypocrisy and inconsistency. Let there be one rule that covers all friends – not one for those with whom you agree and another for those with whom you disagree. For me the better rule is open dialogue among friends on all issues of mutual importance. Under this rule, which President Obama now seems to accept, he should have welcomed Prime Minister Netanyahu's advocacy before Congress, instead of condemning it. He owes Prime Minister Netanyahu an apology, and so do those Democratic members of Congress who rudely stayed away from Netanyahu's informative address to Congress.

CHAPTER 3

THE TRANSITION

November 8, 2016
THE DAY AFTER THE ELECTION

With the world's attention focused on the U.S. presidential election, some attention must be devoted to the problems we will continue to face the day after the election, regardless of who is elected. Here are some of these problems.

1. The world will continue to move away from the center and toward the extremes on both the right and the left. In many parts of Europe – from Poland to Hungary to Greece – neo-fascist parties are strengthening their influence in their governments. In the United States the "alt-right" has been considerably strengthened during this election.

The hard left is also increasing its influence in some part of Europe and on many university campuses. The British Labour Party has now been hijacked by radical extremists on the left. In many universities, the absurd concept of "intersectionality," which has become a code word for anti-Semitism, is dominating discussions and actions by the hard left.

The center is weakening. The empowerment of extremes poses great dangers to the world. The hard right and the hard left have more in common than either has to centrist liberals and conservatives. They both hate America, distrust government, demonize Israel and promote anti-Semitic tropes.

2. Following the election President Obama may try to tie the hands of his successor, regardless of who it may be. During the lame-duck period, when presidents can act without political accountability, he may foolishly send the Israel-Palestine conflict to the United Nations. This would mean the end of the peace process, because the Palestinian would be dis-incentivized from entering into the kinds of direct negotiations without preconditions that the Israeli government continues to offer, and that is the only realistic road to peace. The only hope of stopping

this counterproductive move would be for the President-elect to insist that her or his hands not be tied by the lame-duck president.

(Unfortunately, my concern was ultimately confirmed and President Obama failed to veto the anti-Israel resolution put before the UN Security Counsel, which, besides denying the Jewish people's connection to Jerusalem, dis-incentives the Palestinian leadership from accepting Prime Minister Netanyahu's offer to negotiate without preconditions.)

3. The problem revealed by FBI director Comey's ill-advised statements over the past four months will not end with the election. Comey is a good man, but he has demonstrated an inability to control himself and his agents. The problem of unlawful FBI leaks has become pervasive. It must be addressed by the new administration. Replacing Comey will not be enough, the entire culture of the FBI must be changed and it must be restored to its rightful position as the silent investigative arm of the Justice Department. Indeed, even more fundamental structural changes are now required. The entire Justice Department, of which the FBI is one component, has become too politicized. In most other western democracies, there is a sharp division between the Minister of Justice, who is a political aide to the president or prime minister, and the Director of Public Prosecution, who is a civil servant completely removed from politics. Only the Director of Public Prosecution decides who to investigate and who to prosecute. The political minister plays no role in such decisions. But in the United States we merged these two distinct roles into the job of Attorney General. This must change if our system of justice is to be de-politicized.

4. This election has exacerbated the long-standing problem of criminalizing policy differences. We are quick to confuse differences in policy with charges of criminal behavior. During this election both sides accused the other of criminal conduct. I have long railed against this development, whether it involved accusations against Democrats like Hillary Clinton or Republicans like Congressman Tom Delay or Governor Rick Perry. The criminal law must be reserved for willful, deliberate and clearly defined crimes. We are moving away from that understanding and toward a dangerous expansion of the concept of crime in the context of political differences.

5. Finally, the healing process must begin the day after the election. Lincoln's words should be our guide: "With malice toward none, with charity for all." It is unlikely that either the winners or the losers will be

able to avoid malice and extend charity following this most contentious of elections, but it is essential that the loser accept the result and that the winner be gracious. Both Richard Nixon and Al Gore provide somewhat different models of appropriate responses.

This election revealed that there are deep divisions within the American electorate. Some of these divisions are reasonable and indeed desirable. These include differences over economic policies, foreign policies and other political issues. But this election revealed that there are divisions across impermissible lines: racial, ethnic, gender, religious, class, and a willingness to resort to violence. These divisions will be much harder to heal. But the process must begin on the day after the election.

November 13, 2016
WHAT THE US ELECTION TELLS US ABOUT THE PAST, PRESENT, AND FUTURE

The recent election ended in a virtual tie, as did the election of 2000. Approximately half of the voters selected each of the two major candidates. Clinton received almost three million more votes than Trump. Trump received more electoral votes. If 70,000 more of Clinton's popular votes had been cast in Pennsylvania, 120,000 more in Florida, and 15,000 more in Michigan, she would have had more than the 270 needed to win the presidency.

That's how close the election was. I predicted an unpredictably close vote back in August when Clinton was way ahead in the polls. This is what I wrote in my e-book, *Electile Dysfunction*, "Think about the vote on Brexit. Virtually all the polls including exit polls that asked voters who they had voted for – got it wrong. The financial markets got it wrong. The bookies got it wrong. The 2016 presidential election is more like the Brexit vote in many ways than it is like prior presidential elections. Both Brexit and this presidential election involve raw emotion, populism, anger, nationalism (Britain First, America First), class division and other factors that distort accuracy in polling. So anyone who thinks they know who will be the next president of the United States is deceiving themselves.

"To be sure, the Electoral College vote is sometimes less difficult to predict than the popular vote, because it generally turns on a handful of closely contested critical states, such as Ohio, Florida, Pennsylvania, and Virginia.

"But in this election, there could be surprises in states that are usually secure for one party or the other. So even the electoral vote will be more difficult to predict than in previous elections.

"One reason for this unique unpredictability of the unique unpredictability of Donald Trump himself.... Hillary Clinton is more predictable, but her past actions may produce unpredictable results...A final reason why this election is so unpredictable is because the voter turnout is unpredictable."

In an election that was as unpredictable as this and that turned out to be a toss-up, any one of many factors may have determined the outcome. FBI Director James Comey's ill-advised letter to congressional leaders on October 28, telling them, and the voters, that new emails had been discovered that might be "pertinent to the investigation," may well have made the difference.

In a series of TV appearances, I had urged Comey to do what he eventually did: "The FBI knows how to work that fast. They should get 100 FBI agents working 24 hours a day for three days...and in 72 hours at least release something that indicates whether there is anything, whether there is even probable cause. If there is nothing the public has to know that."

I worried that Comey may not have considered the unintended consequences of his letter: "What if his statements about the emails produce a victory for Trump and it then turns out that there was nothing of significance in them? Or that they were merely duplicates of what had already been produced?" And I've urged him to explain the scope of his investigation:

"Silence is no longer an option for Comey...He can't any longer by silence allow his last statement to influence this election. Look how close it's becoming since that statement was made. To have the FBI influence the outcome of an election and then nothing turn up would be an absolute disgrace to democracy."

On Sunday's *CNN Tonight* Don Lemon credited me with predicting what Comey would do: "Alan. To you. You hate to say I told you so, but you told me and everyone who would listen last week that this would happen. That Comey would have to speak out before the election."

Comey did finally speak out, but it may have been too little, too late. Millions of votes were cast between Comey's two statements. Those votes – based on a misperception that the emails were "pertinent" to the investigation – may have made the difference between a Clinton or Trump victory. No one can ever know for certain, but the election was so close, it is highly probable.

So Trump's narrow victory doesn't tell us much about the past or the present. Even if Trump had lost by a narrow margin, the fact that he got nearly 60 million votes would still be significant – as significant as his narrow victory – in telling us about the current mindset of the American people.

But the fact that Trump won tells us a great deal about the future, because a Trump presidency promises to be very different than a Clinton presidency would have been.

A Clinton presidency – coupled with a Republican Senate and House – would have been subject to the checks and balances of our constitutional system of separation of powers. The Trump presidency is not subject to those constraints. Although there has been some gridlock, there is less than what would have existed under a Clinton presidency.

Just as it was impossible to predict this election, it is impossible to predict the precise dimensions of the Trump presidency. If he is smart, he will reach across the aisle, as well as across genders, ethnicities and religions.

A successful president must be different than a successful candidate. Only time will tell whether Trump acts on this historic truth.

In the meantime, the loyal opposition must remain both loyal and opposed to policies and appointments that are inconsistent with our values. We must cooperate when cooperation is warranted, but when it is not, we must use all available lawful options – political, judicial, media, academic and economic – to serve as checks and balances on a president who tries to exceed his authority. This is not the time for liberals or Democrats to become immobilized with despair, nor is it the time for violence or unlawful actions. It is a time to become energized and proactive.

November 17, 2016
HOW TO ASSESS THE BANNON APPOINTMENT

President Elect Trump's appointment of Steve Bannon as his chief strategist has been criticized on the ground that Bannon is an anti-Semite. There are many reasons for opposing the appointment of

Bannon, but anti-Semitism is not one of them. I do not support the Bannon appointment. But neither do I support accusing Bannon of being an anti-Semite, based on the evidence I have seen.

With regard to anti-Semitism, there are three distinct but overlapping issues: (1) Is Bannon personally an anti-Semite? (2) Does his publication, *Breitbart*, promote anti-Semitic views? (3) Do *Breitbart* and Bannon have followers who are anti-Semitic?

From what I can tell, the evidence cited in support of the accusation that personally Bannon is an anti-Semite falls into two categories: first, that his wife testified at a hotly contested divorce proceeding that he did not want his children to go to school with "whiney Jews"; and second, that he ran an article describing Bill Kristol as a "renegade Jew."

Let us consider these items of evidence in order. Senator Harry Reid tried to strengthen the first accusation against Bannon by saying that it appeared in a court document, thus suggesting that it had the imprimatur of a judge. But that is not the case. The claim was simply made by his former wife in a judicial proceeding, thus giving it no special weight. Bannon has rigorously denied making the statement and said that he and his wife were fighting over whether his children should attend Catholic school, rather than a secular school.

On the other side of the ledger is the testimony of Jewish individuals who have worked closely with him for years. These include my former research assistant, Joel Pollak, an orthodox Jew who wears a kippah and takes off all the Jewish holidays. He is married to a black woman from South Africa who converted to Judaism. Joel assures me that he never heard a single anti-Semitic utterance or saw an anti-Semitic action in the four years they worked together. The same is true of numerous other Jewish individuals who work with him, some of whom thoroughly disapprove of Bannon's politics and the way he ran Breitbart, but none of whom have reported any events of anti-Semitism.

The second alleged item of evidence is the following headline that appeared on *Breitbart*: "Bill Kristol: Republican Spoiler, Renegade Jew." I am advised, however, that this article and the headline were written not by Bannon but rather by David Horowitz, a right-wing Jew who was upset with Kristol for his refusal to support Trump. Horowitz deemed that a betrayal of the Jewish people. While I fundamentally disagree with that appraisal and also of the article, I find it hard to characterize Bannon as an anti-Semite because *Breitbart* ran it. *Breitbart* has also personally attacked me, but that doesn't change my views.

I keep an open mind waiting for more evidence, if there is any, but on the basis of what I have read, I think it is wrong to accuse Bannon of one of the most serious forms of bigotry. So I will not join the chorus of condemnation that employs this radioactive term against Bannon without compelling evidence. The Anti-Defamation League has now commendably acknowledged that there is no evidence of anti-Semitism by Bannon: "We are not aware of any anti-Semitic statements from Bannon."

As to whether Bannon promotes the alt-right, and whether the alt-right includes anti-Semites, I think the answer to that is yes. Both Bannon and *Breitbart* have made bigoted statements about Muslims, women and others, which I do not condone. That is why I do not support Bannon, even though I do not think he's an anti-Semite. Bigotry against any group should be disqualifying for high office. But let's put this criticism of Bannon and *Breitbart* into context. *Haaretz* certainly serves as a platform for the alt-left in Israel. Though it features a wide range of commentary, primarily from the center-left, it also features hard-left writers such as Gideon Levy, who supports academic, cultural and economic boycotts against Israel and its "criminal" regime, as well as Amira Hass, who encourages Palestinians to throw stones and engage in "violent resistance" against Israel. These writers have certainly been accused, and with some justification, of promoting hatred not only against the current Israel government, but against the very nature of Israel and Zionism. Their hateful writings are often quoted gleefully by anti-Zionist and anti-Semites.

This is not to compare *Breitbart* with *Haaretz*, but it is to suggest caution in holding a publication responsible for all the views expressed by its writers. To be sure, *Haaretz*'s general orientation tends to be center-left, whereas *Breitbart* is hard-right, but both serve as platforms for extremes on either side. The same can be said of *J Street*, which is a center-left organization which serves as a platform for, and includes among its active members and contributors, BDS supporters, anti-Zionists and opponents of Israel's existence as the nation state of the Jewish people.

Or consider Black Lives Matter, an organization with a commendable goal, that has promoted anti-Semitism by singling out one country for condemnation in its "platform": calling the nation state of the Jewish People an "apartheid" and "genocidal" regime. In an article in *Above the Law*, Joe Patrice attacks me for my critique of Black Lives Matter, claiming that "it's certainly possible someone in the movement also has sympathy for Palestinians." But there is an enormous difference between "sympathy for Palestinians" (which I share) and accusing the entire nation state of the Jewish people of "genocide" (which I believe is anti-Semitic).

Anti-Semitism and anti-Zionism are prevalent both on the hard-right and on the hard-left. The Trump election has brought hard-right anti-Semitism into public view, but the bigotry of the hard-left is far more prevalent and influential on many university campuses, both in the United States and in Europe. A single standard of criticism must be directed at each. We must judge individuals on the basis of their own statements and actions, and we should be cautious in judging publications and organizations on the basis of who they publish, who their audience is and who supports them.

People of good will, Jews and non-Jews, must condemn with equal vigor all manifestations of bigotry whether they emanate from the hard alt-right or hard alt-left. That is why I cannot support Bannon's appointment, even though he is strongly pro-Israel. But that is also why I can't support those on the hard-left who advocate good causes, while at the same time promoting anti-Semitism and the de-legitimization of Israel.

November 29, 2016
DON'T RIP UP THE IRAN DEAL, ENFORCE IT

CANDIDATE DONALD Trump campaigned on the promise that he would rip up the Iran nuclear deal. But now that he is president-elect, he should look hard at the realistic options to keep Iran from ever developing nuclear weapons.

Although I was strongly opposed to the deal — and wrote a book outlining why — I don't think it's now realistic simply to tear the pact to pieces. It was, after all, signed by several other nations, who will still stand by its terms. That means the full sanctions regime could not be restored effectively. Further, ending the agreement would entitle Iran to pursue its nuclear ambitions now rather than once the deal expires.

Finally, though there is evidence of some minor violations, it appears that Iran is currently complying with the core aspects of the deal.[6]

But neither do I agree with the 76 national security experts who have urged the president-elect simply to continue the Obama policy of accepting the deal as now understood by the signatories. That understanding would allow Iran to begin developing nuclear weapons as soon as the inspection regimes end, in a decade or so.

A far better option would be to enforce all the terms of the deal vigorously, including these unequivocal words in its preface and preamble: "Iran reaffirms that under no circumstances will Iran ever seek, develop, or acquire any nuclear weapons."

Iran bound itself to those words when it signed the agreement. The mullahs would probably argue that the words in the preface and preamble are merely hortatory and thus not a binding part of the pact. They could also assert that the sunset provisions in the deal itself apply to that commitment as well. But nothing in the deal authorizes Iran to develop nuclear weapons. Further, it was and is Iran's official policy, repeatedly expressed by its leaders, that its goal in ending the restrictions is to develop peaceful nuclear technologies. Now, the mullahs may well have been lying, but whatever their collective state of mind, the Trump administration should insist that Iran be taken at the words and be bound by the language of the preface and preamble.

Congress also has an important role to play. To ensure that the agreement is carried out in its entirety, including the all-important reaffirmation, lawmakers should pass a resolution authorizing the American president to use force to prevent Iran from ever becoming a nuclear-weapons state.

Passage of such a law would underscore that Iran's reaffirmation never to acquire nuclear weapons is central to US understanding of the deal. As such, it would provide both a deterrent against Iran violating that commitment and an enforcement authorization in the event it does. I

---

6   It is worth noting, that on June 18, 2017, Iran's Revolutionary Guard fired ballistic missiles at Islamic State militants in Syria, signaling a significant uptick in its involvement in that conflict – which is on Israel's northern border. A week later Israel launched an attack on several Syrian targets in response to Syrian projectiles that landed in the Golan Heights. See *Jerusalem Post*, 6/25/17

am confident that there would be enough votes, both in the Senate and House, to pass such a law.

With President Trump in the Oval Office, Iran's leadership would certainly take seriously a US threat to respond militarily if Iran does violate that reaffirmation — particularly if that declared policy is already backed by a use-of-force authorization. Thus the threat alone should provide sufficient deterrence. But if not, then the military option would become operative. This combination provides the best assurances that Iran will not obtain a nuclear arsenal.

When the deal was being considered, President Obama argued that its critics had failed to offer a better alternative. He was wrong; the proposal outlined above was just such an alternative. But Obama's mistake can now be rectified by adopting this constructive alternative to simply accepting or tearing up the deal.

A clear statement by President Trump, backed up by Congressional action, would provide a needed backstop against the deal's worst-case scenario — the development of a nuclear arsenal by Iran — while still preserving its benefits. Without such a firm statement of American policy, the deal as interpreted by the Obama administration will not prevent Iran from obtaining nuclear weapons. In all probability, it would merely postpone that catastrophe for about a decade while legitimating its eventual occurrence. This is an outcome President Trump should not accept.

November 30, 2016

KEITH ELLISON – THE WRONG MAN AT THE WRONG TIME

What should a political party that has just lost its white working-class, blue-collar base to a "make America great again" nationalist do to try to regain these voters? Why not appoint as the new head of the party a radical left-wing ideologue who has a long history of supporting an anti-American, anti-white, anti-Semitic Nation of Islam racist? Such an appointment will surely bring back rust-belt voters who have lost their jobs to globalization and free trade! Is this really the thinking of those Democratic leaders who are pushing for Keith Ellison to head the Democratic National Committee?

Keith Ellison is, by all accounts, a decent guy, who is well liked by his congressional colleagues. But it is hard to imagine a worse candidate to take over the DNC at this time. Ellison represents the extreme left wing of the Democratic Party, just when the party — if it is to win again — must move to the center in order to bring back the voters it lost to Trump. The Democrats didn't lose because their candidates weren't left enough. They won the votes of liberals. The radical voters they lost to Jill Stein were small in number and are not likely to be influenced by the appointment of Ellison. The centrist voters they lost to Trump will only be further alienated by the appointment of a left-wing ideologue, who seems to care more about global issues than jobs in Indiana, Wisconsin and Michigan. Ellison's selection certainly wouldn't help among Jewish voters in Florida, Ohio and Pennsylvania or pro-Israel Christian voters around the country.

Ellison's sordid past associations with Louis Farrakhan — the long-time leader of the Nation of Islam — will hurt him in Middle America, which has little appetite for Farrakhan's anti-American ravings. Recently, Farrakhan made headlines for visiting Iran on the 35th anniversary of the Islamic Revolution where he berated the United States, while refusing to criticize Iran's human rights violations. Farrakhan also appeared as a special guest speaker of the Iranian president at a rally, which featured the unveiling of a float reenacting Iran's detention of 10 U.S. Navy sailors in the Persian Gulf.

In addition to embracing American enemies abroad, Farrakhan has exhibited a penchant for lacing his sermons with anti-Semitic hate speech. Around the time that Ellison was working with the Nation of Islam, for example, Farrakhan was delivering speeches attacking "the synagogue as Satan." He described Jews as "wicked deceivers of the American people" that have "wrapped [their] tentacles around the U.S. government" and are "deceiving and sending this nation to hell." Long after Jesse Jackson disavowed Farrakhan in 1984 as "reprehensible and morally indefensible" for describing Judaism as a "gutter religion," Ellison was defending Farrakhan and the Nation of Islam in 1995 as a role model for African-Americans, calling him "a tireless public servant of Black people, who constantly teaches self-reliance and self-examination to the Black community."

Ellison has struggled to explain his association with Farrakhan and the Nation of Islam. He has acknowledged working with the Nation of Islam for about 18 months to organize the Minnesota delegation to Farrakhan's 1995 Million Man March in Washington. However, Ellison insists that he never joined the Nation of Islam and more recently, he has held himself out as a friend of the Jewish people and of Israel. This late conversion coincided with Ellison's decision to pursue elected office in Minnesota, and an apparent realization that his association with the Nation of Islam might hurt his political fortunes. In 2006, he wrote a letter to the Jewish Community Relations Council in Minneapolis, in which he apologized for failing to "adequately scrutinize the positions" of Farrakhan and other Nation of Islam leaders. "They were and are anti-Semitic, and I should have come to that conclusion earlier than I did." In his recently released memoir *My Country, 'Tis of Thee: My Faith, My Family, Our Future*, Ellison writes of Farrakhan:

"He could only wax eloquent while scapegoating other groups" and of the Nation of Islam "if you're not angry in opposition to some group of people (whites, Jews, so-called 'sellout' blacks), you don't have religion."

Ellison had to know what Farrakhan was saying: everyone else did. Yet Ellison publicly defended this bigot, writing that Farrakhan "is not an anti-Semite," but rather "a role model for black youth." Ellison then subtly went after what Farrakhan repeatedly described as the Jewish-controlled media.

Ellison argued that the accusation of anti-Semitism was the result of "relentless negative propaganda disguised to defame Afro-Americans." He went on to cast blame on the media, controlled by you-know-who: "Black people have no history of using the media, the movie industry or any other propaganda sources, to collectively defame White America. Any student of the media, however, knows all about how the White media has called our very humanity into question."

As a law student at the University of Minnesota, Ellison defended a speech by Stokely Carmichael, in which Carmichael claimed, "Zionists joined with the Nazis in murdering Jews so they would flee to Palestine." Ellison condemned the university president for criticizing Carmichael's anti-Semitic creed by arguing that:

"... the University's position appears to be this: Political Zionism is off-limits no matter what dubious circumstances Israel was founded under; no matter what the Zionists do to the Palestinians; and no matter what wicked regimes Israel allies itself with — like South Africa. This position is untenable."

Ellison also chose to affiliate with other radical groups in his career as a political organizer and radio talk show host. In 2000, he appeared at a fundraiser for a convicted domestic terrorist Sara Jane Olson of the SLA who participated in the bombing of two police cars.

Ellison said that Olson was prosecuted for her political beliefs, although she pleaded guilty to possession of explosives with intent to murder. He also praised Assata Shakur — a member of the Black Panther Party, and a convicted cop-killer — and praised Fidel Castro for offering her asylum in Cuba.

Moreover, Ellison himself had engaged in bigotry when he was a law student. A woman who had known him then — she is a liberal Democrat and a person of unquestioned integrity — told me that Ellison had said to her: "I can not respect you because you are a woman and a Jew." Views like that do not easily change, especially when the purported change comes about opportunistically as part of a campaign for Congress in a multi-ethnic district.

Nor has Ellison's tune changed all that much, especially when he has spoken to Muslim groups, even after being elected to Congress. In 2010, for example, at a private fundraiser hosted by the past president of the Muslim American Society, Ellison suggested that America's foreign policy is governed by Israeli interests.

In the audiotape, Ellison is heard as saying...

"The United States foreign policy in the Middle East is governed by what is good or bad for a country of 7 million people. A region of 350 million all turns on a country of 7 million. Does that make sense? Is that logic? Right? When the Americans who trade their roots back to those 350 million get involved, everything changes. Can I say that again?

To the mostly Muslim (and pro-Palestinian) audience, Ellison argues that the strong American support Israel receives is largely the result of lobby groups, such as AIPAC:

We can't allow another country to treat us like we're their ATM. Right? ... Now some of us have affinity for other places around the globe. But whether you're born here or whether you accepted America as your own voluntarily, this is our home. Right? All of our home equally, and we can't allow it to be disrespected because some, by a country that we're paying money to ... It just doesn't make any mathematical sense. But it makes all the sense in the world when you see that that country has mobilized its Diaspora in American to do its bidding in America."

After this audio tape emerged, several groups and individuals rescinded their initial endorsement of Ellison, most notably the ADL called Ellison's statement "deeply disturbing and disqualifying." As its chairman Jonathan Greenblatt explained,

"...his words imply that U.S. foreign policy is based on religiously or national origin-based special interests rather than simply on America's best interests ... Ellison's words raise the specter of age-old stereotypes about Jewish control of our government, a poisonous myth that may persist in parts of the world where intolerance thrives, but that has no place in open societies like the U.S."

In addition, Haim Saban, the head of the Brookings Institute Saban Forum and a leading Democratic fundraiser and contributor, has said:

"If you go back to his positions, his papers, his speeches, the way he has voted [he was one of only 8 Congressmen who voted against funding Iron Dome, which protects Israel civilians against Hamas rocket attacks], he is clearly an anti-Semitic and anti-Israel individual ... Ellison would be a disaster for the relationship between the Jewish community and the Democratic Party."

Ellison was one of only two dozen Congressmen to vote "present" rather than vote for a non-binding resolution "recognizing Israel's right to defend itself against attacks from, reaffirming the United States' strong support for Israel, and supporting the Israeli-Palestinian peace process." And in 2010, Ellison co-authored a letter to President Obama, calling on him to pressure Israel into opening the border with Gaza. The letter describes the blockade of the Hamas-controlled Gaza strip as "de facto collective punishment of the Palestinian residents."

Even beyond Ellison's past associations with anti-American and anti-Semitic bigotry and his troubling current voting record with regard to Israel, his appointment as head of the DNC would be a self-inflicted wound on the Democratic Party at this critical time in its history. It would move the party in the direction of left-wing extremism at a time when centrist stability is required. The world at large is experiencing a movement toward extremes, both right and left. The Democratic Party must buck that dangerous trend and move back to the center where the votes are, and where America should be.

One does not have to agree that Ellison is an anti-Semite, to conclude that his appointment would be a disaster for American and for the Democratic Party.

Why then are Senators Schumer, Warren and Sanders supporting this "disaster," even in the face of White House's resistance to Ellison? Don't they realize that many traditional, centrist Democrats of every religious background will leave the Democratic Party if it is headed by Ellison?

The case for Ellison is weak: The Democrats don't have to pander to the hard left. The case against Ellison is overwhelming. If the Democratic Party is to retain its position as the centrist liberal party that cares about all Americans, it must not appoint Ellison to head the DNC.

NOVEMBER 30, 2016

THE FIRST AMENDMENT IS NOT BROKEN SO LET'S NOT TRY TO FIX IT

Nearly all elected politicians – from the president down to local city counselors – want to criminalize flag burning. No decent American wants to see our flag being desecrated. It's a popular issue and politician glom on to popular issues.

That is why we have a Supreme Court: to prevent elected politicians from compromising unpopular basic liberties, such as freedom of expression for those whose views and actions we despise.

The late Justice William J. Brennan once said that if he saw someone burning his beloved American flag, he would punch him in the mouth, but he wouldn't try to convict him of a crime. I would do neither. But nor would I applaud or join in the disgraceful display of anti-American hate.

The situation with regard to flag burning is exactly where it should be in a democracy: nearly everyone despises flag burners, but the constitution forbids us from making it a crime.

The Constitution would also forbid President-Elect Trump from taking away the citizenship of flag burners.

The Supreme Court has not only held that flag burning is constitutionally protected, but also that citizenship cannot be taken away even if a flag burner could be convicted of a crime. Denial of citizenship based on a criminal conviction has been ruled to be unconstitutional.

So President-Elect Trump is wrong on at least two counts: you can't criminalize flag burning; and you can't take away the citizenship of flag burners.

As President, Trump may have the power to change the constitutional status of flag burning, by appointing justices who agree with the minority in the most recent 5-4 flag burning decision.

The late Justice Scalia was in the majority in that case, and if his replacement takes the minority view, the Supreme Court may change its decision. That would be a serious mistake, because of respect for precedent and because it would open a slippery slope for denying other basic freedoms of expression.

Candidate Trump would seem content with that, since he advocated changing the libel laws to make it easier to sue his critics. But any such change may boomerang against Trump himself, who uses defamation as a political weapon.

If the constitutional rules were loosened, Trump might be subject to defamation actions for calling people crooked, corrupt and other defamatory epithets. Being president doesn't immunize the incumbent from being sued for mouthing off against his opponents.

So let's leave the First Amendment alone. Let flag burners be ridiculed and despised in the court of public opinion. Let's not make martyrs of them by hauling them before our courts of law.

The First Amendment has served us well for two and a quarter centuries. It has protected extremists both on the right and left. Most Americans, when polled, would prefer to ban speech they dislike: "Free speech for me, but not for thee."

If Donald Trump had his druthers, he would interpret the First Amendment to protect what he says and does, while at the same time, permitting the government to punish what his critics – and those with whom he disagrees – say and do. But that is not the way freedom operates. Freedom of speech for anyone is freedom of speech for everyone. And denying freedom, of speech to anyone, has the potential of denying it to everyone.

The First Amendment is not broken so let's not try to fix it. Freedom of expression is a principle that liberals and conservatives alike can and should support. Historically it has always been opposed by extremists on both the right and the left, who have no patience for dissenting points of view.

So President-Elect Trump, please withdraw your tweet, develop a thicker skin for criticism, and stop tinkering with our freedom of expression.

If you ever see someone burning the American flag, don't call the cops and don't punch him in the nose. Just remind him that the flag he is burning is what protects his right to burn that flag.

December 23, 2016

TRUMP WAS RIGHT TO TRY TO STOP OBAMA FROM TYING HIS HANDS ON ISRAEL

The Egyptian decision to withdraw the one-sided anti-Israel Security Council resolution should not mask the sad reality that it is the Obama administration that has been pushing for the resolution to be enacted. The United States was trying to hide its active "behind the scenes" roll by preparing to abstain rather than voting for the resolution. But in the context of the Security Council where only an American veto can prevent anti-Israel resolutions from automatically passing, an abstention is a vote for the resolution. And because of this automatic majority, an anti-Israel resolution like this one cannot be reversed by a future American president. A veto not cast cannot be retroactively cast.

The effect, therefore of the Obama decision to push for, and abstain from, a vote on this resolution is to deliberately tie the hands of President Obama's successors, most particularly President-Elect Trump. That is why Trump did the right thing in reaction to Obama's provocation. Had the lame duck president not tried to tie the incoming president's hands, Trump would not have intervened at this time. But if he had not urged the Egyptians to withdraw the resolution, he would have made it far more difficult for himself to try to bring about a negotiated resolution to the Israeli-Palestinian conflict.

The reason for this is that a Security Council resolution declaring the 1967 border to be sacrosanct and any building behind those boarders to be illegal would make it impossible for Palestinian leaders to accept less in a negotiation. Moreover, the passage of such a resolution would dis-incentivize the Palestinians from accepting Israel Prime Minister Netanyahu's invitation to sit down and negotiate with no preconditions. Any such negotiations would require painful sacrifices on both sides if a resolution were to be reached. And a Security Council resolution siding with the Palestinians would give the Palestinians the false hope that they could get a state through the United Nations without having to make painful sacrifices.

President Obama's lame duck attempt to tie the hands of his successor is both counterproductive to peace and undemocratic in nature. The lame duck period of an outgoing president is a time when our system of checks and balances is effectively suspended. The outgoing president does not have to listen to Congress or the people. He can selfishly try to burnish his personal legacy at the expense of our national and international interests. He can try to even personal scores and act on pique. That is what seems to be happening here. Congress does not support this resolution; the American people do not support this resolution; no Israeli leader – from the left, to the center, to the right – supports this resolution. Even some members of Obama's own administration do not support this resolution. But Obama is determined – after 8 years of frustration and failure in bringing together the Israelis and Palestinians – to leave his mark on the Mideast peace process. But if he manages to push this resolution through, his mark may well be the end of any realistic prospect for a negotiated peace.

One would think that Obama would have learned from his past mistakes in the Mideast. He has alienated the Saudis, the Egyptians, the Jordanians, the Emirates and other allies by his actions and inactions with regard to Iran, Syria, Egypt and Iraq. Everything he has touched has turned to sand.

Now, in his waning days, he wants to make trouble for his successor. He should be stopped in the name of peace, democracy and basic decency.

But it now appears that Obama will not be stopped. Four temporary Security Council members have decided to push the resolution to a vote now. It is difficult to believe that they would have done so without the implicit support of the United States. Stay tuned.

[Addendum]
As predicted, the United States allowed the anti-Israel resolution to be approved by the United Nations Security Council. Votes in favor were cast by Russia, which has occupied Königsberg since 1945, after capturing that ancient German city, ethnically cleansing its population and bringing in hundreds of thousands of Russian settlers; China, which has occupied Tibet and brought in thousands of Chinese settlers; France who occupied and settled Algeria for many years; Great Britain which has occupied and colonized a significant portion of the globe;

and assorted other countries, several of which have horrendous human rights records.

Israel, on the other hand, offered to end the occupation and settlements in 2000-2001 and again in 2008 only to be rebuffed by the Palestinian leadership. But Israel is the only country to have been condemned by the Security Council for an occupation and settlement. This hypocrisy is typical of the United Nations as even our representative acknowledged when she explained why the United States abstained.

Now peace will be more difficult to achieve, as the Palestinians become further convinced that they do not have to accept Netanyahu's offer to negotiate without preconditions.

Thank you, President Obama for completing your 8 years of failed foreign policy with a final blow against, peace, stability and decency.

Congress can ameliorate the impact of this destructive resolution by enacting a statute declaring that the resolution does not represent the United States' policy, which is that peace will not come through the United Nations but only by direct negations between the parties. The law should also prohibit any United States funds to be spent directly or indirectly in support of this Security Council resolution. I suspect that the incoming president will be willing to sign such a law.

December 25, 2016
Obama Pulls a Bait-and-Switch on Anti-Israel Security Council Vote

The Obama administration pulled a bait-and-switch in refusing to veto the recent Security Council resolution against Israel. In attempting to justify its abstention – which under Security Council rules has the same effect as a vote in favor – the administration focuses on "new" settlement building, especially in areas deep into the West Bank.

In her speech to the Security Council, Ambassador Samantha Power explained the administration's vote this way:

"Today, the Security Council reaffirmed its established consensus that settlements have no legal validity.... President Obama and Secretary Kerry have repeatedly warned – publically and privately – that the absence of progress toward peace and continued settlement expansion was going to put the two-state solution at risk, and threaten Israel's stated objective to remain both a Jewish State and a democracy...This resolution reflects trends that will permanently destroy the hope of a two-state solution if they continue on their current course." (emphasis added)

Likewise, Ben Rhodes, Obama's Deputy National Security Advisor, said:

"Netanyahu had the opportunity to pursue policies that would have led to a different outcome today....In the absence of any meaningful peace process, as well as in the accelerated settlement activity, we took the decision that we did today to abstain on the resolution." (emphasis added)

In a press release, the pro-Obama advocacy group J Street welcomed America's abstention, citing a poll showing "that 62 percent of Jewish voters believe the United States should either support or abstain from voting on a United Nations Security Council resolution calling on Israel to stop building settlements in the West Bank." (emphasis added)

And the media – from CNN, to *The New York Times*, to *The Wall Street Journal* – also reported that the resolution was only about the expansion of new settlements.

But the text of the resolution itself goes well beyond new building in these controversial areas and applies equally to historically Jewish areas that were unlawfully taken by Jordanian military action during Israel's War of Independence and liberated by Israel in a war started by Jordan in 1967.

The text of the Security Council Resolution says that "any changes to the 4 June 1967 lines, including with regard to Jerusalem," have "no legal validity and constitutes a flagrant violation under international law." This means that Israel's decision to build a plaza for prayer at the Western Wall – Judaism's holiest site – constitutes a "flagrant violation of international law." If it does then why did President Obama pray there and leave a note asking for peace?

Under this resolution, the access roads that opened up Hebrew University to Jewish and Arab students and the Hadassah Hospital to Jewish and Arab patients are illegal, as are all the rebuilt synagogues – destroyed by Jordan – in the ancient Jewish Quarter of the Old City.

Is it really now U.S. policy to condemn Israel for liberating these historically Jewish areas in Jerusalem? Does Obama really believe they should be made judenrein again, as they were between 1949 and 1967?

If so, why didn't the administration openly acknowledge that it was changing half a century of bipartisan support for Israel's claims to these sacred areas? If not, why did it not demand changes in the language of the resolution to limit it to new building in disputed areas of the West Bank? The Obama administration can't have it both ways. It must now declare where it stands on Israel's right to allow prayer at the Western Wall, access to Hebrew University and Hadassah Hospital, and the repair of destroyed synagogues to the Jewish Quarter.

J Street, as well, has an obligation to its members – many of whom pray at the Western Wall and have deep connections to Hebrew University and Hadassah Hospital and the Jewish Quarter of Jerusalem – to advise them whether the organization supports Israel's abandoning these Jewish areas until Palestinians agree to a negotiated settlement.

The media, as well, should clarify the impact of the resolution beyond new building in the West Bank, so that all Americans will know what their President supported.

President-elect Donald Trump and Congress can make it clear that it is not U.S. policy that all changes "to the 4 June 1967 lines, including with regard to Jerusalem" are in violation of international law. The new president can immediately recognize Jerusalem as the capital of Israel and begin the process of moving our embassy there.

The justification for keeping it in Tel Aviv was not to change the status quo, but that justification no longer exists because this resolution does precisely that: it declares the status quo – the reality on the ground that acknowledges Israel's legitimate claims to its most sacred and historical Jewish areas – to be flagrant violations of international law. Congress can legislate no funding to implement the Security Council's troubling resolution.

If the Obama administration refuses to announce that it supports the language of the resolution that applies to the Jewish areas discussed above, then the entire resolution should be deemed invalid because the U.S. did not cast its abstention – the equivalent of a yes vote – in good faith.

[Addendum]
On June 1, President Trump signed a waiver deferring the moving of the U.S. Embassy to Jerusalem for another six months — an act which the Trump administration conveyed was necessary to better lay the

groundwork for fruitful negotiations. President Trump will have the opportunity to reassess his campaign promise when the waiver is up for reevaluation in December.

December 29, 2016
KERRY'S SPEECH WILL MAKE PEACE HARDER

What if the Secretary of State gave a policy speech and no one cared? Because Secretary Kerry's speech came after its abstention on the Security Council vote, few in Israel will pay any attention to anything he said. Had the speech come before the abstention there would have been some possibility of it influencing the debate within Israel. But following the U.S. abstention, Kerry has lost all credibility with Israelis across the political spectrum.

This is why his speech wasn't even aired live on Israeli TV.

The speech itself was as one-sided as the abstention. It failed to mention the repeated offers from Israel to end the occupation and settlements, and to create a Palestinian state on the West Bank and Gaza: Arafat's rejection of the Clinton-Barak proposals in 2000-2001: and Abbas' failure to respond to the Olmert offer in 2008. To fail to mention these important points is to demonstrate the bias of the speaker.

Kerry also discussed the Palestinian refugees, without even mentioning the equal member of Jewish refugees from Arab and Muslim countries. If Palestinian refugees deserve compensation, why don't Jewish refugees deserve the same?

Finally Kerry seemed to confirm that in his view any changes from the pre-1967 lines would not be recognized without mutual agreement. This means that the prayer plaza at the Western Wall, the access roads to Hebrew University and Hadassah Hospital on Mount Scopus, and the Jewish Quarter of Jerusalem are now all illegally occupied. This is, of course, a non-starter for Israelis. It is also wrong as a matter of history and law. Jordan captured these historically Jewish areas in 1948, when all the surrounding Arab countries attacked the new Jewish nation in an attempt to destroy it. Jordan's illegal occupation and ethnic cleansing of Jews was accompanied by the destruction of synagogues, cemeteries, and schools, and the bringing in of Arab settlers to move into the Jewish homes. When Jordan attacked Israel again in 1967, Israel recaptured these Jewish areas and allowed Jews to return to them. That is not an illegal occupation. It is a liberation.

By failing to distinguish between settlement expansion deep into the West Bank and reclaiming historical Jewish areas in the heart of Jerusalem, Kerry made the same fundamental error that the Security Council resolution made. Moreover, equating Jewish Jerusalem with Amona and other Jewish settlements deep in the West Bank plays into the hands of Jewish hard right extremists who also believe there is no difference between Jerusalem and Judea-Samaria: both are equally part of the historic Jewish homeland. Kerry thinks they are equally illegal; the right-wing extremists believe they are equally legal. Both wrongly believe they are equal.

Kerry's one-sidedness was also evident in his failure to press the Palestinian leadership to accept Netanyahu's open offer to begin negotiations immediately with no preconditions. Instead, he seemed to justify the Palestinian unwillingness to enter into negotiations now.

Kerry's pessimism about the two-state solution poses the danger of a self-fulfilling prophecy. The existing settlements — even if expanded — do not pose any danger to the two-state solution, if the Palestinians really want their own state more than they want there not to be a Jewish state. A contiguous Palestinian state is certainly possible even if all the existing settlements were to remain. Israel proved that in Gaza when it dismantled every single Jewish settlement and evacuated every single Jew from the Gaza strip. It is simply a historical geographical and logical error to assume that continuing settlement building – whether one agrees with it or not, and I do not – dooms the two-state solution. To the contrary, settlement expansion is the consequence of the Palestinian refusal to accept repeated offers from Israeli governments to end the occupation and settlements in exchange for peace.

The primary barrier to the two-state solution remains the Palestinian unwillingness to accept the U.N. resolution of 1947 calling for two states for two peoples – the Jewish people and the Arab people. This means explicit recognition by Palestinians to accept Israel as the nation state of the Jewish people. Kerry did not sufficiently address this issue.

The most important point Kerry made is that the Obama administration will not unilaterally recognize a Palestinian state, without an agreement between Israel and the Palestinians. He also implied that the U.S. will not push for any additional Security Council resolution.

Kerry's speech is therefore just that: a speech with little substance and no importance. It will be quickly forgotten along with the many other one-sided condemnations of Israel that litter the historical record.

Kerry would have done a real service to peace if he had pressed the Palestinian leadership to come to the negotiation table as hard as he pressed the Israeli leadership to end settlement expansions. But his one-sided presentation did not move the peace process forward. Let us hope it does not set it back too far. What a missed opportunity – a tragedy that could have been easily averted by a more balanced approach both at the Security Council and with the Kerry speech.

I hope the Trump administration will understand, and act on, the reality that the real barrier to peace is the unwillingness of the Palestinian authority to sit down and negotiate with Israel, with each side making painful compromises, and both sides agreeing to end the conflict once and for all.

December 31, 2016

BRITAIN AND AUSTRALIA MORE SUPPORTIVE OF ISRAEL THAN OBAMA AND KERRY

When the British Prime Minster and the Australians Foreign Minister both criticize the Obama administration for being unfair to Israel, you can be sure that something is very wrong with what President Obama and Secretary Kerry have been doing. This is what Theresa May said:

"We do not believe that it is appropriate to attack the composition of the democratically elected government of an ally. [W]e are also clear that the settlements are far from the only problem in this conflict. In particular, the people of Israel deserve to live free from the threat of terrorism, with which they have had to cope for too long."

This is what Julie Bishop, the foreign minister of Australia, said in explaining why Australia would not have voted for the U.N. Security Council resolution:

"In voting at the UN, the [Australian] Coalition government has consistently not supported one-sided resolutions targeting Israel."

And these are only the *public* criticisms. In *private* several other countries have expressed dismay at the problems caused by the last minute moves of the lame duck Obama administration.

Initially, *The New York Times* failed to report these important international developments, presumably because they disagree with them. Only after other media featured the British and Australian criticism did they decide to cover it. They *did* immediately report that the Jewish community – both in the United States and Israel – is divided between right-wing Jews who oppose the Obama administration's moves and liberal Jews who support them. This is simply fake news: Israel is *not* divided over the Security Council's resolution and the Kerry speech. All Israeli leaders and the vast majority of its citizens opposed these developments. This is true even of the Israeli leftists and centrists who are critical of Israel's settlement policies. The same is true with regard to American Jews, despite *The New York Times* reporting to the contrary. Many liberal Jews and non-Jews, including Senators Schumer, Blumenthal, Gillibrand, and Wyden have been vocally critical. So have numerous liberal congressmen and pundits. I certainly count myself as a liberal Democrat, who opposes Israel's settlement policies, but who is strongly critical of the Obama/Kerry moves.

Only *J Street* – which carries Obama's water – has expressed support, along with a few handfuls of hard-left reform rabbis and professional Israel bashers, who the *Times* reporter quoted as if they were representative of the larger Jewish community.

In contrast to the relative uniformity of Israel's leaders and citizens in opposition to the Obama/Kerry initiatives, the Obama administration itself and the Democratic Party are divided.

Most who have expressed views have been critical, but we have not yet heard from several leading Democrats, especially Keith Ellison who is seeking the chairmanship of the DNC. This is an issue on which silence is not a virtue. It is important for all Democrats to stand up and be counted.

There *is* actually some good news growing out of the Kerry speech. Arab leaders have expressed support for his proposal, which would require the Palestinian Authority to recognize Israel as a Jewish state (or as I prefer to put it, "the nation state of the Jewish people.") Despite this implicit support for such recognition from Arab leaders, the Palestinian Authority adamantly persists in refusing to recognize Israel's Jewish character.

This is the phony excuse Hanan Ashwari, the official spokesperson for the Palestinian Authority, gave for why it would be "against our principles" to recognize Israel as the nation state of the Jewish people:

"If you want to give religion to states, then this is against our principles. I don't recognize Islamic states. I don't recognize Christian states. I don't recognize Jewish states. A state is a state for all its citizens. It has to be Democratic, inclusive, tolerant, and has to be genuinely representative of all its people. You cannot give added value to any people because of their religion or ethnicity."

This statement may win the award for Ashwari as hypocrite of the year. The Palestinian Authority, which she officially represents, has the following in its Constitution:

"Islam is the official religion in Palestine.... The principles of Islamic Shari'a shall be the main source of legislation."

Moreover, the Palestinian Authority recognizes Iran, Saudi Arabia, Egypt, and Jordan, which are all countries that define Islam as their state religion and discriminate against non-believers in their particular brand of Islam.

Is Ashwari really saying that the principles of the Palestinian Authority require it to renounce their own Constitution and to withdraw recognition from all their Muslim allies? What about from Great Britain, which has an official state religion? If so, I challenge her to say that explicitly!

Israel is the only state in the Middle East that grants religious equality to all its citizens as a matter of law. Israeli Arabs enjoy more rights than do Arabs (let alone Jews) of any Arab state. They serve in all branches of government, including the Knesset and the Supreme Court. They have their own religious authorities recognized by the state.

Contrast this to the Palestinian leadership that has vowed that "not a single" Israeli Jew will be able to reside in the future Palestinian state. Furthermore, Israeli Jews are banned from Palestinian universities and other institutions.

So let's have three cheers for Great Britain and Australia, a cheer and a half for Arab leaders, and a big raspberry for the hypocrisy of Hanan Ashwari and her Palestinian Authority.

January 10, 2017
DOES THE ANTI-NEPOTISM STATUTE PRECLUDE TRUMP FROM APPOINTING KUSHNER?

The controversy over President-Elect Trump's expected appointment of his son-in-law, Jared Kushner, to the role of senior advisor raises serious constitutional issues regarding the separation of powers. Congress, which holds the purse strings, may have the power to withhold the salary of a relative who the president wants as an advisor. But it is doubtful whether Congress has the constitutional power to preclude the president – who heads the executive branch – from appointing whomever he chooses as a White House advisor. This is because the separation of powers limits the authority of any one branch to dictate to another branch how it shall conduct its government business. Accordingly, the Supreme Court of the United States does not feel bound by Congressional enactments regarding the recusal of judges for conflict of interest, or other rules of ethics enacted by Congress to constrain its judicial activities. The question of when one branch intrudes on another is often a matter of degree, but each branch guards its independence jealously.

This constitutional issue may never reach the courts for three reasons. First, no one may have standing to challenge such a presidential appointment, especially if taxpayer money is not being spent on his salary. Second, the anti-nepotism statute can reasonably be interpreted to preclude only the *payment* to relatives and not any pro bono service they may render. Third, the statute can be, and has been, interpreted as not applying to White House staff.

There are two relevant provisions of the anti-nepotism statute that was enacted following President John Kennedy's appointment of his brother Robert to be Attorney General. The first prevents "public officials" from promoting a "relative" "to a civilian position in the agency in which he is serving or over which he exercises jurisdiction or control." The second provides that "[a]n individual appointed... in violation of this section is not entitled to pay." There is an apparent conflict between these two provisions since the first appears to provide for an absolute prohibition against the appointment of relatives, whereas the second provides that if the relative is appointed he/she cannot be paid.

In interpreting this poorly drafted statute, a court would have to decide whether Congress intended to prevent only the evil of relatives being paid for jobs for which they have been appointed by their kin, or whether Congress was actually trying to prevent presidents from seeking the advice and council of relatives. A court considering this statute, in the context of a constitutional argument based on separation of powers, might well interpret it narrowly to preclude only the payment of salaries. It might also find it inapplicable to White House staff members, who are not part of any "agency." Indeed, one court, in considering Hillary Clinton's appointment by her husband to direct the White House campaign for health care, suggested that the statute did not apply to White House advisors.

Courts generally interpret statutes, particularly those that are as unclear as this one, in a manner that avoids difficult constitutional questions. So I am relatively confident that President-Elect Trump's appointment of his son-in-law Jared Kushner to be a senior adviser in the White House will not be successfully challenged.

Nor should it be, as a matter of sound policy. Surely our chief executive should have the power to surround himself with anyone he believes, rightly or wrongly, can render sound advice. There are, of course, risks in the appointment of relatives. It would be more difficult for the president to fire his son-in-law – the husband of his daughter and father of his grandchildren – than it would be to fire a non-relative. But that is a factor any president should take into account in hiring a relative. I see no great institutional dangers in allowing such appointments and I do see institutional dangers in prohibiting them.

No statute could, of course, preclude a president from seeking and relying on the advice of relatives. The only question is whether the relative can receive a formal – and in this case non-paying – appointment. There are advantages to a formal appointment: it requires the appointee to avoid conflicts of interest; and it promoted visibility and accountability.

So let the president appoint his son-in-law to this important position as senior advisor and let's all hope, for the benefit of the country, that it is wise decision. History has certainly judged President Kennedy positively for appointing his brother as Attorney General. The two of them worked closely together to end the Cuban missile crisis, to promote civil rights, and to carry out other policies that benefitted the entire nation. The statute should be amended to permit the appointment of relatives, while maintaining the prohibition on the government paying them. That would avoid the evil of financially motivated nepotistic appointments, while preserving the benefits of allowing presidents to choose advisors who they believe will be loyal and beneficial in serving the country.

January 15, 2017
OBAMA'S MIDEAST LEGACY IS ONE OF TRAGIC FAILURE

The Middle East is a more dangerous place after eight years of the Obama presidency than it was before. The eight disastrous Obama years follow eight disastrous George W. Bush years, during which that part of the world became more dangerous as well. So have many other international hot spots.

In sum, the past 16 years have seen major foreign policy blunders all over the world, and most especially in the area between Libya and Iran — that includes Israel, Egypt, Syria, Iraq, Lebanon, Turkey and the Gulf.

With regard to the conflict between Israel and the Palestinians, the Obama policies have made the prospects for a compromise peace more difficult to achieve. When Israel felt that America had its back — under both Presidents Clinton and George W. Bush — they offered generous proposals to end settlements and occupation in nearly all of the West Bank.

Tragically, the Palestinian leadership — first under Yasser Arafat and then under Mahmoud Abbas — did not accept either offers from Israel's Prime Minister Ehud Barak and Clinton in 2000-2001, nor Prime Minister Ehud Olmert's offer in 2008. Now they are ignoring current Prime Minister Benjamin Netanyahu's open offer to negotiate with no preconditions.

In his brilliant book chronicling the American-Israeli relationship, *Doomed to Succeed*, Dennis Ross proves conclusively that whenever the Israeli government has confidence in America's backing, it has been more willing to make generous compromise offers than when it has reason to doubt American support.

Obama did not understand this crucial reality. Instead of having Israel's back, he repeatedly stabbed Israel in the back, beginning with his one-sided Cairo speech near the beginning of his tenure, continuing with his failure to enforce the red line on chemical weapons use by Syria, then allowing a sunset provision to be included in the Iran deal, and culminating in his refusal to veto the one-sided UN Security Council resolution, which placed the lion's share of blame on the Israelis for the current stalemate.

These ill-advised actions — especially the Security Council resolution — have dis-incentivized the Palestinian leadership from accepting Netanyahu's offer to sit down and negotiation a compromise peace. They have been falsely led to believe that they can achieve statehood through the United Nations, or by other means that do not require compromise.

The Iran deal, while it delayed Iran's acquisition of nuclear weapons, virtually guaranteed that it would be allowed to develop a nuclear arsenal as soon as the major restrictions on the deal expire in the next decade. Israel will never allow a regime sworn to the destruction of the nation-state of the Jewish people to secure such a weapon.

So the likelihood of an eventual dangerous military confrontation has been increased, rather than decreased, by the poorly negotiated Iran deal.

Obama's failure to carry out his red-line threat against the Syrian regime's use of chemical weapons has weakened American credibility among its allies and adversaries alike. It has created a power vacuum that Russia was quick to fill. Turkey, too, has flexed its bullying muscles, as its irascible and egomaniacal leader has used the excuse of the Islamic State in Iraq and Syria (ISIS) to go after another American ally, the Kurds, who have at least as strong a claim to statehood as the Palestinians.

America's traditional allies in the Middle East — Israel, Egypt, Saudi Arabia, the United Arab Emirates and Jordan — have all been weakened by Obama's policies, most especially the Iran deal. America's traditional enemies — Iran, Syria and Hezbollah — have been strengthened, along with Turkey.

Terrorism has increased and moved northward to Europe, partly as a result of the Syrian crisis. ISIS, al Qaeda, the Taliban and other terrorist offshoots, though weakened, remain a serious threat to regional stability and to civilians.

A destabilized Middle East poses increasing dangers to American allies and to peace. The blame for this instability is shared by Presidents George W. Bush and Obama. The invasion of Iraq and the overthrow of Saddam Hussein divided that country, rendering it ungovernable, and invited Iran to play a major role in its current destabilized condition.

The toppling of Moammar Gadhafi left Libya open to increasing terrorist influences. The attempt to replace Bashar Assad has turned Syria into a nightmare.

The forced resignation of Hosni Mubarak initially placed Egypt under the control of the Muslim Brotherhood, and strengthened Hamas in the Gaza Strip. Only a coup, opposed by the Obama administration, restored some semblance of stability to Egypt.

Lebanon has become a wholly-owned subsidiary of Hezbollah, a terrorist group under the influence of Iran has an estimated 150,000 missiles aimed at Israel's population centers. The "Shiite arc" now runs from Iran through parts of Iraq and Syria and into Lebanon.

This is the tragic legacy of the Obama administration's failed efforts to undo the harms caused by the George W. Bush administration. Radical Islamic terrorists have replaced authoritarian secular tyrants.

Both are bad, but tyrants at least produce a degree of stability and predictability. They also tend to keep their tyranny domestic, whereas terrorists tend to export their evil tactics.

We should have learned the lesson from the replacement of the tyrannical Shah of Iran by the far more tyrannical and dangerous ayatollahs. But we did not. We insisted on supporting the "democracy" of the Arab spring, which resulted in the replacement of undemocratic domestic tyrants by undemocratic international terrorists.

History will look kindly on Obama's domestic successes, but it will judge his Mideast policy harshly.

CHAPTER 4

THE TRUMP PRESIDENCY

February 1, 2017
IS SALLY YATES A HERO OR A VILLAIN?

Acting Attorney General Sally Yates was fired by President Donald Trump because she instructed the Justice Department lawyers not to defend Trump's Executive Order regarding travel to the U.S. by people from certain Muslim countries. She is neither a hero, nor a villain. She made an honest mistake when she instructed the entire Justice Department not to defend President Trump's wrong-headed executive order on immigration. The reasons she gave in her letter referred to matters beyond the scope of the attorney general. She criticized the order on policy grounds and said that it was not "right." She also referred to its possible unconstitutionality and unlawfulness. Had she stuck to the latter two criteria she would have been on more solid ground, although perhaps wrong on the merits. But by interjecting issues of policy and directing the Justice Department not to defend any aspect of the order, she overstepped her bounds.

An Attorney General, like any citizen, has the right to disagree with a presidential order, but unless it is clear that the order is unlawful, she has no authority to order the Justice Department to refuse to enforce it. This order is multi-faceted and complex. It raises serious constitutional and legal issues that deserved nuanced and calibrated consideration from the nation's highest law officer. There are significant differences between the constitutional status of green card holders on the one hand, and potential visitors from another country who are seeking visas. Moreover, there are statutory issues in addition to constitutional ones. A blanket order to refuse to defend any part of the statute is overkill. If she strongly disagreed with the policies underlying the Order, she should have resigned in protest, and left it to others within the Justice Department to defend those parts of the Order that are legally defensible.

I, too, disagree, with the policy underlying the order, but I don't immediately assume that any policy with which I disagree is automatically unconstitutional or unlawful.

The President has considerable constitutional authority to control entry into the United States by non-citizens and non-residents. Congress, too, has some degree of control over our borders. The precise relationship between presidential and congressional power has never been defined by the Supreme Court. A more responsible Attorney General would seek to analyze these complex issues before jumping into the political fire by a blanket refusal to defend any part of the order.

In addition to failing to do her duty as Attorney General, Sally Yates handed President Trump an underserved political victory. She gave him the power to control the situation by firing her, instead of herself maintaining control by resigning in protest. It is the President who emerges from this unnecessary confrontation with the undeserved status of hero among his constituents.

I do not know Sally Yates except by reputation. She is highly regarded as a career prosecutor and public servant. My criticism of her is not personal, but rather institutional. These are dangerous and delicate times, and anyone who wants to confront the newly elected president must do so with wisdom, nuance and calibration. She played directly into his hands by responding to an overbroad order with an overbroad response. President Trump has now appointed a new acting Attorney General who will defend the order, or at least those parts of it that are legally defensible. Any individual Justice Department official who feels uncomfortable defending this controversial order should be given the freedom by the Department to decline to participate in the case. There are plenty of good lawyers in the Department who would have no hesitation standing up in the courtroom and making the best ethically permissible argument in defense of the order. I have had many experiences with Justice Department lawyers who personally disagreed with the prosecutorial decision in particular cases, but who vigorously defended the government's position.

Sally Yates did what she thought was right. In my view, she was wrong. She should neither be lionized nor accused of betrayal. Nor should President Trump's critics, and I include myself among them, accuse him of doing anything even remotely close to President Nixon's infamous "Saturday night massacre." Nixon fired the very officials who were seeking to prosecute him. That constituted a personal and unethical conflict of interest. President Trump fired Yates over policy differences. It may have been unwise for him to do so, but it was clearly within his authority.

Now we will see our adversarial system at work. Excellent and dedicated lawyers will continue to bring challenges throughout the country against this ill-advised executive order. Other excellent lawyers will defend the order vigorously in court. That is the way our system of checks and balances is supposed to work.

February 2, 2017
ASK NEIL GORSUCH ABOUT MERRICK GARLAND

PRESIDENT TRUMP'S NOMINATION of Judge Neil Gorsuch gives Senate Democrats an opportunity to put a difficult question to the nominee: Does he believe that Senate Republicans acted constitutionally and properly in preventing President Obama's Supreme Court nominee, Merrick Garland, from receiving a hearing or an up and down vote? Gorsuch will try desperately to avoid answering that embarrassing question. [My prediction, in fact, proved to be true. Justice Gorsuch avoided the question stating at the Senate hearing: "I think it would be imprudent for judges to start commenting on political disputes between themselves or the various branches."]

It is embarrassing because, as a constitutional originalist, he must certainly agree that the Senate has a constitutional obligation either to consent or deny consent to a president's nominee. There is nothing in the Constitution that would allow senators to refuse to perform their constitutional obligation, in the hope that the next president will be of their party. Gorsuch would have to express at least some constitutional concerns about the actions of Republican senators following the death of Antonin Scalia a year ago.

But if Gorsuch were to answer that probing question honestly, he would be challenging the legitimacy of his own nomination. He surely will not want to do that, despite the reality that the Scalia vacancy should have been filled by a qualified candidate nominated by President Barack Obama, who had nearly a year left in his term.

Asking and re-asking that embarrassing question during Gorsuch's confirmation hearings would make good theater. It might also make good politics for the Democrats. But it is unlikely to change the result, since Gorsuch is eminently qualified by his academic and judicial background to serve on the high court.

There is an argument, made early in our constitutional history, that "a party nomination may justly be met with party opposition." The Federalist Papers support the argument that the Senate need not sit back and allow a president to reap partisan political advantage from an appointment to the Supreme Court. This argument might justify the Democratic tactic of fighting fire with fire — obstruction with obstruction. It is unseemly, but it is not without historic precedence or justification.

That approach should perhaps be reserved for a nominee whose confirmation would tip the balance of the Supreme Court dramatically in one direction. This nomination — one conservative originalist judge replacing another — is unlikely to tip that balance. The next vacancy, if it were of a liberal seat, might well change the jurisprudence of the Supreme Court in a way that denies fundamental rights to the most vulnerable Americans. If the nominee to fill that vacancy would dramatically shift the current balance, an ideological confirmation battle might well be justified — and would likely occur.

In that circumstance, there might be enough Democrats — aided perhaps by a handful of centrist Republicans — to block the nomination. For now, however, there do not appear to be even enough Democratic senators who would be willing to filibuster this nomination, thus forcing the Republications to vote to rescind the current rule allowing Supreme Court nominations to be filibustered unless there were 60 votes to end debate.

It is tragic that the constitutional process for nominating and confirming Supreme Court justices has become so politicized. Back in 1932, another Republican president was faced with the responsibility of filling the Supreme Court chair that had been occupied by Oliver Wendell Holmes. When President Herbert Hoover showed his list of prospective candidates to Senator William E. Borah of Idaho — who was known to favor a Western Republican — Senator Borah pointed to the bottom name and said, "Your list is all right, but you handed it to me upside down."

The bottom name was that of Benjamin Cardozo, a Democrat from New York and a Jew — but also the nation's most respected state court judge and a paragon of judicial virtue. President Hoover responded that there were already two New Yorkers and one Jew on the court, but Senator Borah declared: "Cardozo belongs as much to Idaho as to New York [and] anyone who raises the question of race is unfit to advise you concerning so important a matter." The rest, of course, is history. The Cardozo nomination was unanimously — indeed, instantaneously — approved, and Hoover was credited with having "performed the finest act of his career as president."

I don't often wish for a return to "the good old days," but when it comes to selecting Supreme Court justices, there is much to be said for the approach taken by President Hoover and Senator Borah.

[Addendum]
On April 7, Neil Gorsuch was confirmed by the Senate to become the 113th Justice of the United States Supreme Court. When Senate Democrats took the 'Nuclear Option' by resorting to a filibuster, Senate Republicans responded by changing the Senate rules to allow all future Supreme Court nominees to pass through the Senate with a simple 51-vote majority (as opposed to the previous threshold of 60 votes.)

February 9, 2017
COURTS CHECK AND BALANCE TRUMP ON IMMIGRATION

No one can predict how the legal challenges to the Trump executive order on immigration will turn out, but the Supreme Court will now get the last word.

It is important to note, however, that President Trump has, thus far, avoided a constitutional crisis by appealing — rather than defying — an overbroad injunction against his Executive Order issued by a federal judge in Washington state. A panel of the 9th Circuit Court of Appeals refused to rescind the injunction on an emergency basis, thus keeping the nationwide injunction in effect, at least until the court considers briefs from both sides. Another federal judge in Massachusetts rendered a decision refusing to renew a similar injunction, and thus allowing the visa restrictions to be implemented.

In light of these conflicting rulings, the President could have said that he was going to follow the one he and his lawyers believed was correct. Had he done so, the judge in Washington might well have held the President in contempt of court, thus creating a constitutional crisis between co-equal branches of our government.

Instead, Mr. Trump ordered his Justice Department to immediately appeal what he characterized as the "ridiculous" opinion of "this so-called judge," as Mr. Trump characterized Justice James Robart on Twitter Saturday morning. The White House initially characterized the injunction as "outrageous," but then withdrew that injudicious characterization — only to have the President tweet even more injudicious language that may well offend the Appellate Courts to which the order will be appealed.

Justice Robart's order is neither ridiculous nor outrageous, as evidenced by the refusal of these appellate judges to immediately overrule it. And the judge himself, who was appointed by former President George W. Bush, is not "so-called" – he is a respected jurist who rendered what he honestly believed was a proper decision under the law.

Having said that, the Washington injunction is too broad in scope and lacks nuance. It may well be modified on full appeal. It applies equally to individuals with different constitutional status. For example, a family from Yemen, with no connection to the U.S., has no cognizable right to receive a visa, whereas, a visa holder already in this country might have such a right. But if the injunction is upheld, the President will have to comply with it, regardless of his personal views or his lawyers' professional judgments. As the Washington state attorney general correctly put it, "No one is above the law, not even the President."

Whatever one thinks about the merits or demerits of Justice Robart's injunction – or of the Massachusetts federal judge's refusal to renew the injunction – we are observing in action the American system of checks and balances, and separation of powers.

Although the executive and legislative branches are solidly in Republican hands, a single district court judge, representing the lowest level of the judicial branch, can bring a presidential order to a screeching halt – at least until and unless it is reversed or modified on appeal. And there is nothing the President can do about it, other than tweet his outrage and order an appeal to be taken to the Court of Appeals and eventually to the Supreme Court.

But because Republican senators refused to allow former President Barack Obama to fill the vacancy resulting from Justice Scalia's death a year ago, the High Court might well split 4-4 if this case comes before them, as the justices did when a case involving Mr. Obama's executive order on deportation came to them from the federal courts in Texas. A 4-4 split leaves the lower court judgment intact.

But if the plaintiffs appeal the Massachusetts order, the Supreme Court may be presented with conflicting judgments. The 9th Circuit may affirm the granting of the nation-wide injunction, while the 1st Circuit affirms the denial of the injunction. A 4-4 split would leave both conflicting orders in place, thus causing uncertainty and even chaos. That is why the pending nomination of Neil Gorsuch – as the potential tie-breaking ninth Justice – is so important.

[Update: Justice Neil Gorsuch has since been confirmed to the Supreme Court, ensuring that if the High Court grants review, the case will be heard before all nine justices, unless any recuse themselves.]

There are, of course, other options. Mr. Trump could rescind the executive order and re-write it in a more careful and lawful manner. As currently written, it contains several constitutionally questionable provisions, especially with regard to religion. An executive order could be crafted so as to eliminate these questionable elements, without compromising on national security. This would require the kind of consultation with experts – legal, military, intelligence, legislative – that was obviously lacking in the hasty rollout of this broad and unduly provocative order.

If he wants to clean up the mess he caused, President Trump would have to acknowledge that he issued the initial order in haste – that he was wrong. But "wrong" is not a word that comes easily to Donald Trump, at least when he is talking about himself.

So we may have to live with the uncertainty resulting from an overbroad executive order, an overbroad injunction against that order and overbroad appeals from conflicting judicial decisions.

No one ever said that the system of checks and balances, and separation of powers, would be efficient or pretty. But this case demonstrates that, like democracy itself, our complex system of governance is better than its alternatives.

February 9, 2017
ISRAEL MUST NOT CRIMINALIZE POLITICAL DIFFERENCES

I recently returned from a visit to Israel, where the headlines focused on two investigations involving Prime Minister Benjamin Netanyahu. The first is about conversations between the prime minister and Arnon Mozes, the publisher of *Yedioth Ahronoth*, a popular Israeli newspaper. The second concerns gifts of cigars for Netanyahu and pink champagne for his wife from a long-time personal friend. According to news accounts, the prime minister will soon be questioned for the fourth time about the two cases. The first one poses significant dangers to freedom of the press and to democratic governance. The second is an example of a widespread problem in many democracies: namely the effort to criminalize political and policy differences.

I write this article not to defend the incumbent prime minister. I would write it regardless of who served in that office. I have made similar points over many years opposing overzealous criminal investigations of political figures. I have also criticized Republican efforts to turn Hillary Clinton into a criminal for her misuse of a private email server. The criminalization of policy and political differences poses a grave danger to democracy, regardless of who the target of the criminalization happens to be.

These dangers exist when vague laws governing the receipts of gifts from friends are broadened and applied retroactively and selectively to a controversial public official. But they are multiplied when the criminalization extends to the relationship between the media and elected officials. Both freedom of the press and democratic governance require breathing room. Questioning the motives of publishers and politicians chills the exercise of free speech and the independence of legislators.

Journalists should never be questioned by prosecutors or police as to *why* they wrote a particular article, *why* they endorsed a particular candidate or *why* they wrote critically of a politician. Nor should an elected official be questioned about *why* he voted for or against particular legislation or took other political action. To probe the motives of journalists or public officials is to chill the exercise of their freedom.

The U.S. Constitution explicitly provides that no members of Congress may (with limited exceptions) be "questioned" about their votes, speeches or debates by any government officials. And both American and

Israeli law protects journalistic privileges from unwarranted disclosure regarding reportage. These enactments, and others, recognize the importance of allowing legislators and journalists to do the important work of democracy without fear of heavy-handed intrusion by police or prosecutors.

An independent press is essential to democratic checks and balances. The Israeli press has not always been as independent as it should be. In the early years of the state, political parties directly controlled "their" newspapers. Elected officials and party functionaries appointed publishers, editors and reporters – and approved or disapproved what was to be published. It was not thought to be a crime for Prime Minister David Ben-Gurion to demand – explicitly or implicitly – positive coverage of his policies, politics or personal actions as a condition of continued employment by those who worked for his party's newspaper.

Newspapers are now, thankfully, more independent of such direct party control. But the relationship between the media and elected officials is still often based on implicit or explicit quid pro quos. An elected politician is more likely to vote for legislation that may benefit a company, if that company provides him or her positive coverage. Put more directly, many elected officials would be reluctant to vote against legislation that would a favor media company, if they worried that a negative vote might result in negative coverage.

However, it would be unthinkable for prosecutors or police to haul into investigation rooms every journalist or politician whose reporting or voting might have been influenced by self-interest. But that is the implication – or at least the slippery slope – of the current investigation.

The prime minster is essentially being investigated for trying to persuade a newspaper with a long history of attacking him and his family to be fairer. The publisher is being investigated for seeking the enactment of legislation that would curtail his competition. In the end, the prime minster voted against the legislation and the publisher continued the attacks on him and his family.

So what we are left with is an exploration of motives: Did the publisher try to get the prime minister to support the legislation by promising to end or reduce the attacks? Did the publisher believe that the prime minister would actually change his strong opposition to the legislation into strong support? Did the prime minister really intend to change his opposition to support, or was he merely playing him, as politicians do? Did the prime minister actually believe that the publisher would suddenly change his long history of attacks into support? If the prime minster believed he was doing something criminal by discussing these issues, why did *he* record the conversations and not erase the tapes?

These are the kinds of questions that should be left to voters and readers, in deciding for whom to vote and to which newspapers to subscribe. They are not the kinds of questions that prosecutors and police should be empowered to ask elected officials and media moguls as part of a criminal investigation.

The relationship between politics and the media – and between politicians and publishers – is too nuanced, subtle and complex to be subject to the heavy hand of criminal law.

Many votes by politicians are designed, in part — whether consciously or unconsciously — to garner favorable coverage from the media and to achieve other self-serving results. In many cases, a piece published by a reporter, editor or publisher is also calculated to some degree to promote self-interest – whether economic, political or career-related. To empower prosecutors to probe these mixed motivations is to empower them to exercise undemocratic control over crucial institutions of democracy.

Consider the proposed *Israel Hayom* law that is at the center of this investigation. More than 40 Knesset members supported the law, despite its obvious constitutional problems. Did they all do so out of altruistic motivates alone? Or did at least some of them allow the fear of negative or the prospect of positive coverage by *Yedioth Ahronoth* – the main beneficiary of the proposed law – to tip the scale in favorite of their support? Should prosecutors and police be empowered to question under oath every member of Knesset who supported the bill to probe his or her motives? Should they be empowered to question the journalists who subsequently published favorable reports about these supporters?

This is the "parade of horrible" that may follow from the current investigations of the prime minster and the publisher.

In the contemporary political climate, in which large media companies – whether it be *Yedioth*, *The New York Times*, Time-Warner, *Bloomberg*, Fox, Yahoo, Facebook or Google – do more than report the news, there will be more and more regulation of their activities by government.

These media companies will seek to influence the political discourse that affects their bottom line, as they simultaneously report on them.

In some instances, positive votes will be rewarded by positive coverage, negative votes by negative coverage. That is – and always has been and always will be – the nature of politics and its relationship to those institutions that report on it. "Scratch my back and I will scratch yours" is as Israeli as falafel and as American as apple pie.

Voters and readers have the right, perhaps the power, to promote more visibility and accountability from those for whom they vote and whose news they read or view. But police and prosecutors should not intrude on this complex, messy and nuanced relationship between politics and the media, except in cases of clear and unambiguous financial corruption well beyond what is alleged in the current case.

So, whatever your views of Prime Minister Netanyahu or publisher Mozes, think beyond the politics of this investigation and to the dangerous precedents being set by empowering prosecutors, police and even judges to intrude so deeply into the mechanics through which the legislature and the media work. Ultimately, judgment about these institutions and their incumbents must be left to the voters and readers, not to unelected police and prosecutors. That is the way democracy is supposed to work.

February 10, 2017
TRUMP SHOULD RETURN TO THE DRAWING BOARD ON IMMIGRATION ORDER

According to three judges of the U.S. Court of Appeals for the 9th Circuit, legal precedents by the Supreme Court doomed President Trump's Executive Order limiting entry to our country.

This decision creates a conundrum for the Trump Administration. He may very well win if and when the case gets to the Supreme Court, especially if Judge Neil Gorsuch is sitting in the 9th seat.[7] The Circuit Court decision, despite its unanimity, is questionable on the law. It extends Constitutional protections to foreigners who have never been in the United State, have no connections to our country, and have no Constitutional right to come here.

---

7   Update: On April 7, Neil Gorsuch was confirmed as the ninth Justice on the Supreme Court.

Consider a family from Yemen, who apply for a tourist visa and are turned down. They couldn't hire a lawyer to bring a lawsuit in the U.S. and expect to win. The courts would rule that they had no "standing" or viable legal claim. Contrast that with a family already here on an academic visa or with a green card, who are deported or refused re-entry after a trip back to their home country.

They would have standing and a plausible claim that their exclusion violated their constitutional rights.

But the 9th Circuit refused to distinguish these cases, ruling instead that the Executive Order was probably unconstitutional as to all who seek to enter the United States from any of the seven countries originally designated by the Obama Administration.

This ruling went beyond what even the State of Washington asked the Federal District Court to declare unconstitutional. It also extended the concept of standing well beyond existing precedents.

And it interpreted the Establishment Clause of the First Amendment, "Congress shall make no law respecting an establishment of religion" — more broadly than any previous court, relying on campaign rhetoric by candidate Trump and a media interview with Rudy Giuliani.

The bottom line is that the Trump administration would have a good chance to snatch victory from the jaws of defeat, if they can get the Supreme Court to decide the case on its merits. Total victory would not be a certainty even in the High Court, but partial success might well be achieved.

The problem for the Trump administration is that it would take time for the case to reach the Supremes. In the meantime, the Executive Order would remain inoperative as a result of the stay ordered by the District Court and affirmed by the 9th Circuit. It is unlikely, though not impossible, that the stay would be lifted by the Supreme Court or by an en banc decision of a larger number of judges of the 9th Circuit. But if it isn't, the stay could remain in effect for many months. Hence the Trump conundrum.

President Trump has said that enforcing his Executive Order is necessary to protect our national security, "The security of our nation is at stake." He has even gone so far as to claim that if there were any acts of terrorism now, the judges would be to blame.

But that's simply not true. President Trump has the option of re-drafting the Executive Order so as to eliminate its constitutionally questionable aspects, while preserving its most important protective provisions.

A re-drafted order could apply only to people without green cards or other current connections to the United States. It could make other changes as well, which would reduce the likelihood that the court would strike it down.

Issuing a re-drafted order would constitute an implicit admission by the Trump administration that there were problems with the original order. And President Trump is not likely to admit he was wrong. But if he really believes that the security of our nation is at stake, he must put our security before his ego. In his press conference on Friday afternoon, Trump implied that he and his team may be working on a replacement or supplementary order. I have been urging them from day one to follow this route, and I hope they will do so.

So let the current case proceed on its slow track to the Supreme Court, but in the meantime let the President work with the new Attorney General and his national security team to draft a revised order that protects us from terrorism without compromising constitutional rights.[8]

That would be a win-win for all Americans.

February 13, 2017
TRUMP WELCOMES NETANYAHU

Israel's longtime Prime Minister Benjamin Netanyahu will soon be welcomed to the White House by newly elected President Donald Trump. What can we expect from this initial meeting between two strong-willed national leaders?

I know them both – Netanyahu better than Trump – and I believe they will get along well. They are both no-nonsense pragmatists who understand the relationship between economic development and political progress. We all know of Trump's business background and focus on jobs and trade. Less well-known is Netanyahu's business background.

---

8   The Trump administration has since redrafted the executive order. The revised order incorporates important changes such as distinguishing green card holders and other people with connections to the U.S. from those that do not have a visa, and have no clear connection to the United States.

Like Trump, Netanyahu went to business school and began his career as a businessman, working for Boston Consulting Group. When he entered politics, he helped transform Israel from an agrarian-based economy into "start-up nation," which has become a technological superpower with a strong economy. He is the Alexander Hamilton of Israel, to David Ben-Gurion's Jefferson. Trump has to admire that.

Trump will also admire Netanyahu's strong nationalism and love of country. He has made Israel great, militarily, technologically and economically. He may soon become Israel's longest serving Prime Minister, surpassing the legendary Ben-Gurion.

Each leader would like to be the one who succeeds in bringing a peaceful resolution to the Israeli-Palestinian conflict. So many others – people of good will and considerable effort – have been unable to achieve this goal. There is no certainty that Trump and Netanyahu can succeed when so many others have come close but have never been able to close the deal. Both are respected for their deal-making capabilities – Trump in business, Netanyahu in domestic politics.

But there are considerable barriers to achieving a peaceful resolution. Netanyahu and his Palestinian counterpart, Mahmoud Abbas, each have domestic constituencies that would oppose the compromise necessary to achieve a two-state solution. Some of Netanyahu's right-wing coalition partners oppose a two-state solution in which Israel would turn over most of the West Bank to establish a Palestinian state. And many West Bank Palestinians – not to mention Hamas in Gaza – oppose recognizing the legitimacy of Israel as the nation-state of the Jewish people. They also demand the "return" of millions of Palestinian refugees to Israel, despite the reality that there are probably only a hundred thousand or so actual refugees who themselves left Israel in 1948-1949, many voluntarily.

It must be remembered that Israel has twice in recent times offered the Palestinians a state on 95 percent of the West Bank. In 2000-2001, then Prime Minister Ehud Barak and then President Bill Clinton made a generous offer. Yasser Arafat, who was being advised by Jimmy Carter, rejected it and started a violent intifada, in which more than 4,000 people were killed. Then in 2008, Prime Minister Ehud Olmert made an even more generous offer, to which Mahmoud Abbas did not respond. And in 2005, Prime Minister Ariel Sharon unilaterally ended the military occupation and settlements in the Gaza Strip, only to be greeted with thousands of rocket attacks and terror tunnels from Hamas.

Much has changed since these Israeli offers and actions. The current Israeli government is not likely to offer more than what was rejected by the Palestinians. So the pressure must now be placed on the Palestinian leadership to make good faith counter-offers. That pressure can only come from the United States. This is so because the rest of the international community – the United Nations, the European Union, the courts in The Hague, the BDS movement – all dis-incentivize the Palestinians from making compromises, by falsely telling them they can get a state without negotiating with Israel.

President Trump must make it crystal clear that unless the Palestinians negotiate a reasonable solution with Israel, they will never have a state. President Obama did not send that message with clarity, especially when he ordered his United Nations Representative to allow a one-sided anti-Israel resolution to be passed by the Security Council.

President Trump must reassure Prime Minister Netanyahu that he will apply pressure – perhaps through our Sunni allies – on the Palestinian Authority, and not only on Israel, as the Obama administration did. History shows that American administrations that really have Israel's back – not to stab, but to support – are more likely to persuade Israel to offer compromises.

So, I hope that Benjamin Netanyahu will emerge from the White House meeting with the confidence in American support to stand up to those in his cabinet who oppose the two-state solution and who want to expand settlement activity. And I hope the Palestinian leadership will understand that they have no option other than to accept the Netanyahu offer to negotiate anywhere, anytime, and with no preconditions. Perhaps then we will finally see a reasonable resolution to the age-old conflict.

February 17, 2017

TRUMP: PALESTINIANS MUST EARN A TWO STATE SOLUTION

President Trump raised eyebrows when he mentioned the possibility of a one state solution. The context was ambiguous and no one can know for sure what message he was intending to convey. One possibility is that he was telling the Palestinian leadership that if they want a two state solution, they have to do something. They have to come to the negotiating table with the Israelis and make the kinds of painful sacrifices that will be required from both sides for a peaceful resolution to be achieved. Put most directly, the Palestinians must <u>earn</u> the right to a state. They are not simply entitled to statehood, especially since their leaders missed so many opportunities over the years to secure a state. As Abba Eban once put it: "The Palestinians never miss an opportunity to miss an opportunity."

It began back in the 1930s, when Great Britain established the Peel Commission which was tasked to recommend a solution to the conflict between Arabs and Jews in mandatory Palestine. It recommended a two state solution with a tiny noncontiguous Jewish state alongside a large Arab state. The Jewish leadership reluctantly accepted this sliver of a state; the Palestinian leadership rejected the deal, saying they wanted there to be no Jewish state more than they wanted a state of their own.

In 1947, the United Nations partitioned mandatory Palestine into two areas: one for a Jewish state; the other for an Arab state. The Jews declared statehood on 1948; all the surrounding Arab countries joined the local Arab population in attacking the new state of Israel and killing one percent of its citizens, but Israel survived.

In 1967, Egypt and Syria were planning to attack and destroy Israel, but Israel preempted and won a decisive victory, capturing the West Bank, Gaza Strip and Sinai. Israel offered to return captured areas in exchange for peace, but the Arabs met with Palestinian leaders in Khartoum and issued their three infamous "no's": no peace, no recognition, and no negotiation.

In 2000-2001 and again in 2008, Israel made generous peace offers that would have established a demilitarized Palestinian state, but these offers were not accepted. And for the past several years, the current Israeli government has offered to sit down and negotiate a two state solution with no pre-conditions – not even advanced recognition of Israel as the nation state of the Jewish people. The Palestinian leadership has refused to negotiate.

President Trump may be telling them that if they want a state they have to show up at the negotiating table and bargain for it. No one is going to hand it to them on a silver platter in the way that former Israeli Prime Minister Ariel Sharon handed over the Gaza Strip in 2005, only to see it turned into a launching pad for terror rockets and terror tunnels.

Israel must get something in return: namely real peace and a permanent end to the conflict.

The Palestinian leadership's unwillingness to come to the negotiating table reminds me of my mother's favorite Jewish joke about Sam, a 79-year-old man who prayed every day for God to let him win the New York lottery before he turns 80. On the eve of his 80th birthday, he rails against God:

"All these years I've prayed to you every day asking to win the lottery. You couldn't give me that one little thing!" God responded: "Sam, you have to help me out here – buy a ticket!!"

The Palestinians haven't bought a ticket. They haven't negotiated in good faith. They haven't accepted generous offers. They haven't made realistic counter proposals. They haven't offered sacrifices to match those offered by the Israelis.

Now President Trump is telling them that they have to "buy a ticket." They are not going to get a state by going to the United Nations, the European Union or the international criminal court. They aren't going to get a state as a result of BDS or other anti-Israel movements. They will only get a state if they sit down and negotiate in good faith with the Israelis.

The Obama Administration applied pressures <u>only</u> to the Israeli side, not to the Palestinians. The time has come – indeed it is long past – for the United States to tell the Palestinians in no uncertain terms that they must negotiate with Israel if they want a Palestinian state, and they must agree to end the conflict, permanently and unequivocally. Otherwise, the status quo will continue, and there will be only one state, and that state will be Israel.

The Palestinians are not going to win the lottery without buying a ticket.

February 24, 2017

I WILL LEAVE THE DEMOCRATS IF KEITH ELLISON IS ELECTED ITS CHAIRMAN

Tomorrow the Democratic National Committee (DNC) will have to choose the direction of the Democratic Party, as well as its likely composition. It will be among the most important choices the DNC has ever had to make.

There has been powerful push from the hard-left of the Democratic Party, led by Sen. Bernie Sanders (I-Vt.), to elect Rep. Keith Ellison (D-Minn) chairman. If he is elected, I will quit the party after 60 years of loyal association and voting. I will become an independent, continuing to vote for the best candidates, most of whom, I assume, will still be Democrats. But I will not contribute to the DNC or support it as an institution.

My loyalty to my country and my principles and my heritage exceeds any loyalty to my party. I will urge other like-minded people — centrist liberals — to follow my lead and quit the Democratic Party if Ellison is elected chairman. We will not be leaving the Democratic Party we have long supported. The Democratic Party will be leaving us!

Let me explain the reasons for this difficult decision.

Ellison has a long history of sordid association with anti-Semitism. He worked with and repeatedly defended one of a handful of the most notorious and public anti-Semites in our country: the Reverend Louis Farrakhan. And worked with Farrakhan at the very time this anti-Semite was publicly describing Judaism as a "gutter religion" and insisting that the Jews were a primary force in the African slave trade.

Ellison has publicly stated that he was unaware of Farrakhan's anti-Semitism. That is not a credible statement. Everyone was aware of Farrakhan's anti-Semitism. Farrakhan did not try to hide it. Indeed, he proclaimed it on every occasion. Ellison is either lying or he willfully blinded himself to what was obvious to everyone else. Neither of these qualities makes him suitable to be the next chairman of the DNC.

But the connections are more recent as well. In 2009, Ellison headlined a fundraiser for Esam Omeish, a former candidate for Virginia state delegate who had told Palestinians that "the jihad way is the way to liberate your land."

Ellison's voting record with regard to Israel is among the very worst in Congress. Ellison is now on an apology tour as he runs for DNC chairman, but his apologies and renunciations of his past association with anti-Semitism have been tactical and timed to his political aspirations.

He first claimed to realize that Farrakhan was an anti-Semite when he ran for office in 2006 seeking Jewish support. His claim to be a supporter of Israel was timed to coincide with his run for the chairmanship of DNC. I do not trust him. I do not believe him. And neither should centrist liberal supporters of Israel and opponents of anti-Semitism.

The DNC has a momentous choice this weekend. It can move the party in the direction of Jeremy Corbyn's Labour party in England, in the hope of attracting Jill Stein Green Party voters and millennials who stayed home. In doing so they would be giving up on any attempt to recapture the working class and rust-belt voters in the Midwestern states that turned the Electoral College over to Donald Trump.

I do not want to see the Democratic Party relegated to permanent minority status as a hard-left fringe. There is no reason to think the country has moved so far to the left that the Democrats can win by pushing even further in the direction of the hard left. The self-destructive election of Keith Ellison will be hard to undo for many years.

So, tomorrow, the Democrats must choose between electing Ellison or keeping centrist liberals, who support Israel, like me and many others in their party. I hope they choose wisely. But if they do not, I have made my choice.

February 27, 2017
ELLISON WAS DEFEATED BY HIS OWN ACTIONS, NOT BY ANY SMEAR

The close vote by the Democratic National Committee to reject Keith Ellison as its chairperson was a victory for basic decency and a defeat for the kind of bigotry represented by Ellison's past associations with Louis Farrakhan and his current voting record against Israel's Iron Dome. Ellison's loss is not attributable to any "smear campaign," as some of his supporters have falsely alleged, but rather to his own actions, both past and present. Would anyone call it a smear if a candidate's history of sexism, racism or homophobia had been exposed? Why then is it a smear to have raised questions based on Ellison's past associations with anti-Semitism and his current anti-Israel voting record? Nor was it a smear to question Ellison's credibility when he said that he was not aware that Farrakhan was an anti-Semite, when Farrakhan himself was publicly boasting about his Jew hatred.

The smear charge itself reflects the kind of double standard within elements of the Democratic Party that worry centrist pro-Israel voters. Both Democrats and Republicans alike must have the same zero tolerance for anti-Semitism as they do for sexism, racism and homophobia.

The growing influence of intolerant hard left extremists endangers both our country and the Democratic Party. Democrats must recognize the reality that the United States is not a hard left country. Unlike some European countries, we have never had significant Communist or socialist parties. Nor are we a hard right country, with a history of fascist parties. We govern from the center, alternating centrist liberals, such as Obama and Clinton, with centrist conservatives like the Bushes and Reagan.

When the Democrats tried to move leftward, even with such moderate leftists as McGovern, Mondale and Dukakis, they have been overwhelmingly defeated. The combined electoral votes of these three leftish candidates would not have been enough to win a single election. The Republicans experienced similar rejection when they went to the far right of their party and nominated Barry Goldwater.

Had Sanders won the Democratic nomination, he would have won no more than a handful of states. It is far easier for the hard left fringe of the Democrats to win primaries and conduct loud demonstrations than to win national or state wide elections. If the Democratic Party fails to understand this reality they will emulate the British Labour Party, which rejected the kind of moderate liberal leadership represented by Tony Blair in favor of the extreme leftist Jeremy Corbyn. The Corbyn led Labour Party is popular among left wing extremists.[9]

Great Britain has a far greater proportion of hard left voters than the United States. Yet even there, the radical Corbyn left may not be able to attract enough voters to win a majority— even in the post Brexit environment. It would be worse— much worse – for the Democrats if they become the party of the extreme left.

Those who believe that Democrats can win by attracting the kind of hard left radicals who voted for Green Party candidates such as Jill Stein or Ralph Nader are blinking reality. The Democrats could never nominate a winning candidate far left enough for those hard left ideologues to abandon their extremist candidates. Extremists like Susan Sarandon

---

9 In Britain's most recent election held in June, Corbyn's Labour Party outperformed most polls and predictions, gaining a total of 262 parliamentary seats and unseating many of their Conservative political opponents. By contrast, the Conservative Party – under Prime Minister Theresa May – lost eight seats and scrambled to form a coalition government.

seem to believe that a vote for Trump will hasten the revolution. This is how she put it: "Some people feel that Donald Trump will bring the revolution immediately if he gets in, things will really explode."

Nor can the Democrats win by emulating the tactics of the Republican Party. The Tea Party did move the Republicans to the right by their uncompromising and obstructionist approach. But the United States has more tolerance – unfortunately in my view – for rightward movement (as long as it's not too extreme) than the Democrats have for leftward movement.

The current leadership of the Democratic Party is reacting short term to a long-term problem. They are responding to the loudest, shrillest and most demanding voices – voices that are hardly representative of the tens of millions of voters they will need to remain competitive in upcoming races.

The Democrats can win only by regaining their traditional base among working class rust belt voters they lost to Trump. These voters will never support the kind of radical left wing candidates promoted by the Keith Ellison wing of the party.

Ellison's appointment as the deputy to Tom Perez – the man who defeated him – elevated unity over principle. His past history and current voting record should have disqualified him for any office within the Democratic Party. But despite that unfortunate appointment, I will remain in the Democratic Party and work from within to move it back to its vibrant liberal center and away from its radical fringe. I will also work to maintain bipartisan support for Israel and against efforts by the hard left to abandon the only democracy in the Middle East.

It will be a daunting task but it is worth the effort. We won the fight against Ellison, though it was close. We must continue to win if the Democratic Party is to remain competitive.

March 10, 2017
Cuba, 60 Years Later

I finally made it to Cuba – nearly 60 years after first trying. It was Christmas vacation during my senior year at Brooklyn College. Five members of Knight House – the poor folks version of a live at home fraternity at my commuter college –decided to visit Havana. Our motives were not entirely pure. Yes, we wanted to see the old City of Havana and its cultural gems. But we had also wanted to participate in its notorious nightlife. We were 20 years old and seeking post-adolescent adventures of the sort we couldn't experience back in Brooklyn.

We never made it. When we got to the Miami airport for the half-hour, $50 flight, we were greeted by a State Department travel advisory. It seems like another young man – just a dozen years older than we were – was also trying to get to Havana. He had been trying for several years and finally – on the very day we were departing Miami for Havana – Fidel Castro and his revolutionary army were at the outskirts of the city

Disappointed, we returned to Miami Beach where we had to be satisfied with Jai Alai and crowded beaches. Years later I learned that members of a rival house plan, undeterred by a mere "advisory," had taken the flight to Havana and partaken of its vices – vices which were soon to end, or be driven underground by Castro's revolution.

The disappointed young man who didn't make it to Cuba in 1958 is now an old man, with different tastes and tamer vices, such as an occasional cigar and a Cuba Libra drink. Among my passions now are art and music, and Cuba excels at both. So my wife and I, with three other couples, set out on an age-appropriate adventure as part of a "people-to-people" cultural group. Travelers still need an acceptable "justification" to visit the long-boycotted destination. Mere tourism or the love of beaches won't do. It has to be cultural, religious, educational or some other broad category of virtuous pursuit. You still can't go there for the reasons we had in mind back when Castro had kept us involuntarily virtuous.

So we went to visit the studios and houses of Cuban artists – some established, others young and on the way to achieving international recognition. The visits were fascinating, as the artist regaled us with stories of their own experiences with increasing artistic freedom, as Cuban artists became part of the international art market. This made some of them quite rich, at least as compared with average wages for other occupations including lawyers and doctors.

The artists also told us of the increasing acceptance of homosexuality, which had been criminalized and repressed by Fidel Castro. (Interestingly, even during the worst periods of anti-gay repression, the American hard left rarely criticized Castro because he, too, was hard left.) Now, Raul Castro's daughter is leading a movement for equal rights for gay Cubans.

Other positive changes were also visible. Tourism is thriving, and tour guides are among the growing middle class, along with homeowners who rent out apartments to tourists. With tourism comes increasing capitalism and freedom of communication. We heard a diversity of views, including some critical ones, from Cubans we encountered. But we sensed some remaining constraints on full freedom of expression.

On Friday night, some of us attended a beautiful Shabbat service at the local synagogue. There was no Rabbi, so the service was led by a group of teenage visitors from Argentina. The dining room table was set for 80 expected guests, who would feast on chicken and other delicacies not easily available to most locals. The woman who heads the Jewish Community proudly described a recent visit to the synagogue by Raul Castro, who she said had a warm spot in his heart for Jews, if not for Israel, with which Cuba has no formal relations.

Tourist resorts and restaurants are filled, and the food – mostly continental with a Cuban influence – is quite good. Prices are reasonable, compared to large U.S. cities, but unaffordable to all but a select few locals.

The nightlife is vibrant, with Las Vegas-type spectacles at the old Flamingo, as well as jazz at bars. The 1950s mafia controlled hotels – The National, and others like it – have been refurbished and made ready for the anticipated influx of American tourists, as travel restrictions are lifted.

On the negative side, the effects of the failed communist economy were evident. Beautiful old buildings – many of them architectural gems – were in disrepair, some of them crumbling.

The Cuban people suffered from the excesses of exploitive mafia influenced authoritarianism under Fulgencio Batista, and then from the excesses of tyrannical communism under Fidel Castro. What the future holds is uncertain, but to this American visitor, it feels like the Cuban people may be somewhat better off today than they were under either extreme. They still have a long way to go.

March 13, 2017

HOW TO MAKE THE RUSSIA-TRUMP INVESTIGATION BIPARTISAN

With Attorney General Jeff Sessions recusing himself from the Russia-Trump investigation, it is likely that the investigation will be conducted by Sessions' associates at the Justice Department.[10] Even if those conducting the investigation are entirely objective, many Americans will not trust an investigation conducted by individuals whose careers will depend on approval by their recused boss, Jeff Sessions. Nor will the public necessarily trust a special prosecutor appointed by the Republican controlled Justice Department.

Neither will the public have confidence in investigations conducted by Republican dominated congressional committees. The minority party lacks the power to issue subpoenas or call witnesses, so any investigation is likely to be skewed in the direction of Republican interests.

The ideal investigatory body would be a bipartisan commission as the kind appointed following 911, but it is unlikely that any such commission will be appointed, despite the fact that all Americans – Democrats and Republicans alike – are affected by Russian intrusion into our elections.

I have come up with an alternative that, while not perfect, assures that there would be bipartisan input into an investigation of the Russian-Trump connection. Under this alternative, investigations could be conducted by <u>state</u> attorneys general in states that voted for Trump but that have Democratic attorneys general.

One such state is Pennsylvania, where polls had Clinton in the lead, but Trump eventually won by seven-tenths of one percent. The attorney general of Pennsylvania is a brilliant and accomplished lawyer and a Democrat who recently won election despite the Trump victory. He has the power to conduct investigations, subpoena witnesses and documents, and even indict if criminal conduct is established. Nor would any such investigation by a state attorney general intrude on the legitimate authority of the federal government.

Recall that our presidential elections are really 50 state elections for electors. If Russia improperly interfered with the presidential election in an effort to make Trump the president, it is reasonable to assume that their interference may well have had an impact on the Pennsylvania presidential election for its 20 electors. Surely the attorney general of the state should have the power to investigate whether any such interference with <u>its</u> voters may have occurred.

---

10   The investigation into reported ties between the Trump campaign/
administration and Russia has since been overseen by Deputy Attorney General,
Rod Rosenstein, and the special counsel that he appointed, Robert Mueller.

In a McCarthy era case, the United States Supreme Court ruled that federal law pre-empted states from prosecuting individuals for treason-like offenses, such as sedition. That decision and others that followed it, would not, in my view, preclude states from conducting investigations regarding the impact of any Russian interference on the election of their electors.

An investigation conducted by the attorney general of Pennsylvania, or by the attorneys general of the hand full of other states that voted for Trump but have Democratic attorney generals, would not be easy to conduct. Out of state subpoenas would have to be issued. Out of state witnesses—even some in foreign countries –would have to be questioned.

Privileges would be claimed by government officials, both domestic and foreign. Some of these barriers would also stand in the way of any Justice Department or Congressional investigation but the barriers would be somewhat more difficult – though not necessarily impossible – to overcome by a state attorney general.

On the positive side, a well-conducted state investigation would serve as a check and balance on investigations conducted by Republican controlled investigatory agencies. An investigation by Democratic attorneys general would help assure that the other investigations did not become partisan whitewashers.

State attorneys general are becoming increasingly important in serving as checks and balances against the Republican controlled executive and legislative branches of our national government. The lawsuit brought by the attorneys general of Washington and Minnesota forced the president to change and reissue his executive order regarding immigration. State attorneys general should begin to flex their legal muscles in a quest of bipartisan justice.

An investigation into the Russia-Trump affair by state attorneys general would be a worthy sequel to the lawsuits brought against the Trump immigration order by the attorneys general in Washington and Minnesota.

March 16, 2017
WHY THE SUPREME COURT WILL UPHOLD TRUMP'S TRAVEL BAN

Here we go again. Two federal judges have struck down the key provisions of President Trump's revised travel ban. There will be more to come, as constitutional challenges are brought to courts around the nation.

This time there will be no revised new executive order. The president will stick with this one and have his Justice Department appeal it, first to the circuit courts and then the Supreme Court.

President Trump cited my statements on television in support of his prediction that the Supreme Court would rule in his favor:

"Even liberal Democratic lawyer Alan Dershowitz — good lawyer – just said that we would win this case before the Supreme Court of the United States."

I did say that, even though I do not support the ban as a matter of policy. There is a difference, of course, between a law being bad policy and being unconstitutional. Oliver Wendell Holmes once described the role of the lawyer as making "prophecies of what the courts will do in fact." But as Yogi Berra once quipped "it's tough to make predictions, especially about the future." It's even harder if the prediction is about what nine justices will rule in a given case.

Having said that I will venture a prognostication: I think the justices will uphold the major provisions of the order, if the case gets to them. It may not, because the order is a temporary ban that may expire before it reaches the High Court, thereby making the case moot.

If the case reaches the Supreme Court, a major issue will be whether campaign rhetoric delivered by Donald Trump, when he was a private citizen running for president, may be considered by the courts in deciding on the constitutionality of an executive order. The lower courts gave considerable, indeed dispositive, weight to these anti-Muslim statements in deciding that the travel ban was, in reality, a Muslim ban that would violate the constitutional prohibition against discrimination on the basis of religion.

Under that reasoning, had the identical executive order been issued by President Obama, it would have been constitutional. But because it was issued by President Trump, it is unconstitutional. Indeed, any executive order issued by President Trump dealing with travel from Muslim countries would be constitutionally suspect because of what candidate Trump said. In my view, that is a bridge too far. It turns constitutional analysis into psychoanalysis, requiring that the motives of the president be probed.

Most political leaders have mixed motives underlying their actions: they want to protect the security of the nation; they want to appeal to their political base; they want to keep campaign promises; they want to win.

Trump campaigned on the pledge that he would specifically address the issue of "Islamic Terrorism" — a term President Obama refused to use. Trump believes that radical Islam is the major source of the terrorist threat faced by the U.S. It would follow from this view, that the countries that pose the greatest danger of allowing terrorists to reach our shores are countries that sponsor terrorism and do not vet their citizens for terrorist ties.

Most prominent among these nations is Iran, which is the largest promoter of terrorism and which has targeted and continues to target the United States. It is entirely natural to include "The Islamic Republic of Iran" on any list that is designed to deal with terrorism. The same is true, to varying degrees, of the five other predominantly Muslim countries on the Trump list: Syria, Yemen, Sudan, Somalia and Libya.

The fact that all these countries are predominantly Muslim — indeed, most have established Islam as their official state religion — does not suggest religious discrimination. Those are the very countries that pose the greatest danger of terrorism, in the view of the Trump administration. They are not the only such countries, but if others were added to the list, they too would be predominantly Muslim countries.

But what about France or Belgium or England? They too have experienced Islamic inspired terrorism. But these countries have far better vetting procedures. It is not a coincidence that when the Obama administration devised a list, for a different but related purpose, of countries that posed a risk of unvetted terrorists, it was the identical list initially employed in the original Trump travel ban.

When Willie Sutton was once asked "why do you pick banks to rob," he replied "because that's where the money is." Not all the money, but enough of it to prioritize banks.

Similarly, when asked why these six countries were prioritized, the Trump administration responds, "because that's where the terrorists are," — not all of them but these countries aren't vetting them properly.

The inclusion of the six Islamic countries in the travel ban is rational. It may not be the best list. Perhaps there should be no country list at all. But that is a judgment allocated by Congress and the Constitution to the executive branch. It is subject, of course, to the constraints of the Constitution. But the judicial branch will generally defer to the executive branch on matters involving national security, unless there is a clear violation of the Constitution.

In my opinion, that high threshold has not been reached in this case. So I predict the Supreme Court, if it gets the case, will find the new executive order constitutional.

March 16, 2017
THE RIGHT TO CHOOSE INCLUDES THE RIGHT TO CHOOSE LIFE

There is no conflict between the "right to choose" and "the right to life" in the context of abortion, because the former includes the latter. If the state were ever to require a pregnant woman to undergo an abortion – as China in effect did with its "one child" policy – there would be a conflict. But in the United States, the right to choose includes the right to choose life rather than abortion. It also includes the right of women to choose abortion for themselves.

So, what are the anti-abortion right-to-life advocates complaining about? They do not want any woman to have the right to choose abortion for herself. They want to have the state choose for her – to *deny* her the right to choose between giving birth to an unwanted child and having an abortion.

They believe that abortion is infanticide – murder – not of their child but of the fetus of the woman who would choose abortion. But that woman does not regard the fetus as her child. So, the right to lifer responds: it doesn't matter what *you* think. It matters what the *state* thinks. The vast majority – 70% – of citizens in the United States think a woman should have the right to control her own reproduction – to choose whether the embryo or the fetus becomes her child, according to a Pew study this year.

If a woman has been impregnated while being raped, she may not regard the fetus as "her child." The same may be true of other unwanted pregnancies, such as those of teenagers who mentally and physically may be unable raise or care for a child for the rest of her life. The problem is what the late Senator Daniel Patrick Moynihan called, "Children having children."

What gives other people the right to decide, when they are not the ones who will have to bear the consequences?

So, the issue is not *whether* there should be choice, but rather *who* should make the choice. What is more than ironic that so many conservatives, who believe that the state should not make *other* choices for its citizens, insist on the state making *this* highly personal choice for all women.

Right-to-life extremists argue, of course, that *no one* has the right to make *any* choices that will result in the destruction of an embryo or fetus. It is *their* business, they insist, to prevent the pre-meditated "murder" of *every* potential life, even that being carried by a stranger, who honestly believes that her unwanted fetus is not yet a "life" – at least for the first trimester or so – unless she chooses to give birth to it.

These right-to-lifers would go so far as to require a young girl who was raped by her drunken father to bear that child. It is not the fetus's fault, they would argue, that it was created by incestuous rape. Let it not be killed for the sin and crime of the father.

Those right-to-lifers who would make an exception in such extreme cases – and most elected officials who claim to be right-to-life advocates *do* support limited exceptions – must acknowledge that they are supporting the right of the pregnant girl, rather than the state, *to choose* whether to abort or give birth. Why then should other pregnant females who have compelling reasons – medical, emotional, familial, religious, financial – not have the right to choose? Why should the impersonal state take that right from them?

The issue of "who decides?" is a complex one in a democracy governed by the rule of law and the separation of powers. In addition to the personal question, we must also ask the jurisprudential question: "Who decides who decides?" Is it the legislators in our 50 states who decide whether it is the state or the individual who gets to make the choice? Is it the members of Congress? Is it a majority of the nine Supreme Court justices?

This is not an easy question, even for those of us who strongly support a woman's right to choose, as a matter of morality, justice or religion. Not every moral or religious right is a constitutional right, enforceable by the Supreme Court. There is nothing explicit in our Constitution regarding abortion. There are vague references to the right of individuals to be "secure in the persons," which imply a right of privacy. But there are equally vague references to the right to "life." Any honest reading of the words, history and intended meaning of the Constitution, must lead to the conclusion that the framers did not consider the issue of abortion. They did not explicitly include either the right to choose or the right to life in the context of the abortion debate: it was not occurring at the time of the framing. But the framers almost certainly did include the power of future courts to give contemporary meaning to the open-ended words they selected for a document they hoped would endure for the ages – as it has done.

In 1973, the Supreme Court did interpret the Constitution to accord pregnant women a right to choose abortion, at least under some circumstances. This decision *Roe v. Wade* was not the Supreme Court's finest hour with regard to constitutional interpretation. Many scholars, including me, criticized its reasoning and methodology. But it has become the law of the land. Over the past 44 years, it has been slightly changed by subsequent cases, but its core has remained the same; a pregnant woman has the right to choose whether to abort the fetus or give birth to the child. The debate continues around the edges: when *does* "life" begin? When, during the course of a pregnancy, *does* the right to choose end? But at its core the right of a woman to choose – abortion or life – remains solidly ensconced in our jurisprudence.

March 17, 2017

A SUPPORTER OF ISRAEL MUST HAVE A "BIAS" ON TRUMP TRAVEL BAN: THE NEWEST BIGOTRY!

A recent panel discussion regarding the Trump travel ban was infected by the bigotry of one of the participants. The host, Don Lemon, called on former prosecutor, John Flannery, to express his views on the decision of a federal judge to stay the order. This was Flannery's response:

"...Here's Trump saying that we have to write rules. What have they been doing? They've been sitting on their hands doing nothing this entire time. And our dear colleague, Alan Dershowitz, I think, hopes that this may secure Israel and thinks that this is a bogus argument..."

I asked him what he was talking about, since in my dozens of TV appearances discussing the travel ban, I have never once mentioned Israel, and certainly never made the argument that the ban – which I oppose as a matter of policy – would "secure Israel."

He replied: "I think that's what you believe."

I shot back: "I never said a word about Israel. You know when you focus everything I say on Israel it really raises questions about your own bigotry and bias."

I then asked him directly "what does this have to do with Israel? Why... do you have to bring in Israel to attack me and criticize me? Is it because I'm Jewish? You know your bigotry is showing?"

He then said it has "everything" to do with Israel. He insisted that Israel is the "reason you're taking the position you are. Because of your own bias."

The "position" to which he was referring is my view that although the travel ban is bad policy, it is probably not unconstitutional. Instead of responding to my "position" on the merits, he again – quite irrelevantly – repeated that he doesn't think the ban "will help Israel."

Having heard variations on this argument many times in my debates about a wide range of issues – that my loyalty to Israel clouds my judgement and disqualifies me as an objective critic – I really tore into him: "You can't believe anything I say because I'm a Jew and a Zionist? For shame on you sir." I then announced that I don't want to be on panels with him in the future.

At the end of the segment Don Lemon asked if anyone wanted to "apologize" or explain if they feel they "were taken out of context."

Flannery chimed in: "I have trouble understanding you Alan, in connection with this argument about the appeal...we have an honest disagreement about that."

I responded: "my only criticism of you was that you raised the issue of Israel and somehow questioned my motives because yes, I'm a Jew who supports Israel."

There was no legitimate reason for Flannery to bring Israel into the discussion. At no point during my analysis of Trump's revised travel ban – and I have spoken on this issue broadly both on TV and in print – did I suggest that this executive order relates to Israel, let alone would "secure" her. In suggesting that the reason for my position on the travel ban is "because of [my] own bias" toward Israel – and by doubling down on this position throughout the segment – Flannery engaged in an old trope: that one's dual loyalty undercuts their objectivity when it comes to analysis of domestic political issues here in the United States. By morphing the discussion about the constitutionality of U.S. immigration policy into a polemic against me and my pro-Israel "bias," Flannery displayed his own bias.

I'm glad I called Flannery out on this issue. I don't know generally what his views are about Israel. But his willingness to argue to an international TV audience that I am biased on the travel ban issue <u>because</u> I see every issue through the lens of my pro-Israel views is dangerous if unrebutted. The reality is that the U.S. travel ban has little or nothing to do with Israel, but in Flannery's distorted mind it has "everything" to do with Israel if expressed by a Jewish supporter of Israel.

There is an old joke about a European student who was obsessed with Jews. Every time the professor gave an assignment, the student would find a way to bring in the Jews. Finally, in exasperation, he assigned the students to write an essay on the Pachyderm. The obsessed student handed in his essay, with the title: "The Elephant and the Jewish Question."

March 23, 2017
HOLOCAUST DENIAL AND THE MARKETPLACE OF IDEAS

Anyone who wants to understand the current spate of fake news and fake history must go back some years to its most extreme modern manifestation: Holocaust denial. An entire industry has been built to legitimize Holocaust denial. The deniers have funded "research" "institutes," "journals," books, magazines, videos, websites, newsflashes – all designed to provide a patina of academic respectability to demonstrable falsehoods. Nearly every day, I receive dozens of emails from websites with such legitimate-sounding names as "The Institute for Historical Review," "Legalienate" and "Reporters Notebook" that purport to disprove "the Holocaust yarn." These include newsflashes containing "new facts" that put the "final nail in the coffin of history's

Mother of all hoaxes" – that Jews were "allegedly gassed" and cremated at Treblinka and other "death camps."

This entire denial enterprise is devoted to proving that the Holocaust – the systematic murder of more than six million Jews in gas chambers, and via mass shootings, mobile killing units and other means of implementing the carefully planned genocide – simply did not occur; that it was made up wholesale by "The Jews" for financial and political gain. To Holocaust deniers, it matters not a whit that many of the hands-on perpetrators publicly admitted to their crimes and provided detailed eye-witness trial testimony. Nor does it matter that extensive documentation was maintained by the fastidious Nazi murderers. Even the surviving physical evidence is explained away by deniers who are unconcerned with truth. "There were no gas chambers", the deniers insist, echoing Groucho Marx's famous line "Who are you going to believe – me? Or your lying eyes?"

No reasonable person with a modicum of intelligence can actually believe that Hitler and his Nazi co-conspirators did not plan the implementation of the policy of mass extermination of Jews at the Wannssee Conference in 1942, and that they did not carry it out at death camps, such as Treblinka, Chelmno, Majdanek and Auschwitz-Birkenau, as well as by SS mobile killing units that gathered Jews in such places as Babi Yar and the Ponary Woods. During a recent visit to the Polish town from which my father's family had emigrated I learned of the fate of two teenage relatives: a sixteen-year-old girl who was taken as a sex slave by Nazi soldiers and then murdered, and her fifteen-year-old brother who was murdered in Birkenau. They were among dozens of my father's and mother's relatives who were victims of the Nazi genocide. The evidence of the Holocaust is beyond any dispute.

Yet, thousands of people, many with academic degrees, and some with professorial positions, persist in denying the undeniable. These professional liars were given a degree of legitimacy by Noam Chomsky, who not only championed the right of these fake historians to perpetrate their malicious lies, but who actually lent his name to the quality of the "research" that produce the lies of denial. A widely circulated petition of 1979, signed by Chomsky as well as Holocaust deniers such as Serge Thion, Arthur Butz and Mark Weber, described the notorious denier Robert Faurisson as "a respected professor" and his false history as "findings" based on "extensive historical research," thus giving it an academic imprimatur. Chomsky has since argued that he had intended only to support Faurisson's right to free speech and not the validity of his claims, but whatever his intentions may have been, his name on the petition helped to bolster not only Faurisson's standing, but also that of Holocaust denial.

I, too, support the right of falsifiers of history to submit their lies to the open marketplace of ideas, where all reasonable people should reject them. The First Amendment to the United States Constitution does not distinguish between truth and lies, at least when it comes to historical events. Just as I defended the rights of Nazis to march through Skokie, and the right of Ku Klux Klan racists to burn crosses on their own property, I defend the right of mendacious Holocaust deniers to spin their hateful web of lies. But, unlike Chomsky, I would never dream of supporting the phony methodology employed by liars such as Faurisson, by saying it is based on "extensive historical research." Chomsky should be praised for defending the right of Holocaust deniers, but he should be condemned if his involvement in the petition lent substantive and methodological credibility to their false history.

The marketplace is one thing, but let me be clear that I do not believe that any university should tolerate, in the name of academic freedom, these falsehoods being taught in the classroom. There is not and should not be academic freedom to commit educational malpractice by presenting provable lies as acceptable facts. Universities must and do have standards: no credible university would tolerate a professor teaching that slavery did not exist, or that the Earth is flat. Holocaust denial does not meet any reasonable standard deserving the protection of academic freedom.

This is not to say that outside the classroom, academics should be limited in their research output, or prevented from publishing improbable claims. Several years ago, I had a case that tested the proposition that professors had the right to publish what their colleagues believed was "false" information. My client, a distinguished Harvard Medical School professor of psychiatry, had examined numerous patients who claimed to have been abducted by space aliens. He then wrote a book in which he said that on the basis of what he had heard from his patients, he could not exclude the possibility that some of them may have actually experienced alien abductions. He did not teach his theory in the classroom or assign the book, which became an instant bestseller, turning him into a talk show celebrity. Harvard was not amused. The Dean of Harvard Medical School appointed a faculty committee to investigate his "astounding" claims about the possible reality of alien abductions. I came to his defense and posed the following question: "Will the next professor who is thinking about an unconventional research project be deterred by the prospect of having to hire a lawyer to defend his ideas?" Eventually the professor was cleared but the controversy persisted.

It still does, both on university campuses and in the political sphere. Where should the line be drawn between demonstrably false facts and controversial matters of opinion? Should professors be allowed to teach that there are genetic differences between blacks and whites that explain disparities in outcomes? (A Nobel-prize winning Stanford Professor of Engineering tried to teach such a course on what he called "dysgenics.") Should the president of a university be allowed to speculate in public about possible genetic differences between men and women regarding the capacity to do groundbreaking work in maths and science? (Harvard's former President Lawrence Summers lost his job over that.)

I have no problem with courses being taught about the phenomenon of Holocaust denial – it is after all a widespread concern – just as I would have no problem with courses being taught about the phenomenon of false history, false facts and conspiracy theories. But the classroom, with its captive audience of students being graded by professors, is never an appropriate place to espouse the view that the Holocaust did not take place. By publishing his book, the psychiatry professor mentioned above placed it in the public sphere, where readers could choose whether to read it, and believe its claims, or not. The classroom, however, is not a free and open marketplace of ideas. The monopolistic professor controls what can and cannot be said in his or her closed shop. Accordingly, the classroom must have more rigorous standards of truth than the book market, or the internet.

The responsible media should behave in a similar fashion to the professor in the classroom. They should report on the phenomenon of Holocaust denial but not themselves publish unsubstantiated claims that the Holocaust did not occur. There is no way to impose such standards on the free-wheeling internet, where Holocaust denial is rampant. It isn't clear whether the apparent recent surge in online Holocaust denial has been caused by an increase in deniers, or whether closet deniers now have public platforms or social media that they previously lacked.

How then does this all relate to the current phenomenon of false political news and facts? How should the media, academics and the general public deal with politically motivated accusations that the "news" or "facts" they publish are false? Should they report on news and facts asserted by politicians that they have fact-checked and found to lack credibility? How should they deal with deliberately fake news circulated by social media to make a point? Who, in a free and open democratic society, is the judge of whether news, facts, history or other forms of expression are false, true – or somewhere in between? Do we really want governmental (or university) "truth squads" empowered to shut down stalls that are purveying false goods in the marketplace of ideas? And if not, what are the alternatives?

Censorship is, of course, a matter of degree, with the worst being governmental prior restraint, or criminalization of dissent. Following that would be university denial of academic freedom to express unpopular views outside the class. Then there is refusal by the media to report on events or issues out of fear of losing readership or advertising revenue. Finally there is self-censorship, based on fear of violating community norms.

The government – particularly the executive and legislative branches – must be kept away from the daunting task of striking the appropriate balance between free speech and the dangers it may pose, because dissent against the state must remain the paradigm of protected speech. The courts will inevitably have to play a role in striking that balance, but should invoke a heavy presumption in favour of free speech. The university administration should maintain reasonable standards, in the classroom and hiring decisions, but it must not interfere with the right of faculty and students to express unpopular or even "false" ideas outside the classroom. And the media should articulate and enforce reasonable journalistic standards in reporting and fact-checking on information that some claim is false. In the unregulated world of the internet and social media, there will neither be universal standards nor all-encompassing censorship. There are no "publishers" or censors in the cyber world. In the end, the people will decide what to believe, what to doubt and what to disbelieve. And they will not always make wise determinations in a world where lies spread with far greater speed than ever before.

There is no perfect solution to this dilemma. I have hanging on my wall a letter written in 1801 by the then President Thomas Jefferson in response to a pamphlet that would have criminalized the expression of opinions that were deemed to be dangerous to good order and morality. Jefferson criticized the call for judicial censorship arguing that if "the line is to be drawn" by judges, "the conscience of the judge then becomes the standard", and "will totally prostrate the rights of conscience in others." He believed that "We have nothing to fear from the demoralizing reasoning of some, if others are left free to demonstrate their errors."

I wish he were correct about having "nothing to fear" from the open marketplace of ideas, but history has shown that "demoralizing reasoning" and false facts are too often accepted by many, even when others "demonstrate their errors". The reality is that freedom of speech is anything but free. It can be hurtful and dangerous. It can provide a platform and a megaphone for false news and facts.

Freedom of speech and the open marketplace of ideas are not a guarantee that truth, justice or morality will prevail. The most that can be said is that freedom of expression is less bad than its alternatives such as governmental censorship, official truth squads or shutting down the marketplace of ideas. Like democracy itself, untrammelled freedom to express hateful and dangerous lies may be the "worst" policy – except for all the others that have been tried over time.

April 12, 2017
SPICER'S MISTAKE AND THE DEMOCRATS' OVER-REACTION

Sean Spicer made a serious mistake when he compared Bashar Al-Assad to Hitler, and to make matters worse, he got his facts wrong. He quickly and fully apologized. There was no hint of anti-Semitism in his historical mistake and his apology should have ended the matter. But his political enemies decided to exploit his mistake by pandering to Jews. In doing so, it is they who are exploiting the memory of the six million during the Passover Holiday.

The Democratic National Committee issued a rebuke with the headline "We will not stand for anti-Semitism." Its content included the following: "Denying the atrocities committed by Adolf Hitler and the Nazi regime is a tried and true tactic used by Neo-Nazis and white supremacists groups that have become emboldened since Donald Trump first announced his campaign for president." By placing Hitler and Trump in the same sentence, the DNC committed a mistake similar to that for which they justly criticized Spicer. Moreover, the DNC itself, is co-chaired by a man who for many years did "stand for anti-Semitism" – namely Keith Ellison, who stood by the notorious anti-Semite Louis Farrakhan, while denying that he was aware of Farrakhan's very public Jew-hatred. It is the epitome of Chutzpah for the DNC to falsely accuse Spicer of standing by anti-Semitism while it is they who are co-chaired by a man who committed that sin. In another display of Chutzpah, Jeremy Ben Ami of *J Street*, an organization that supports Keith Ellison, characterized Spicer's statement as "unforgivable." I do not recall him saying that Ellison's collaboration with a notorious anti-Semite was "unforgivable." Indeed, Ben Ami quickly forgave him and continues to support him.

Nancy Pelosi, the House Minority leaders, falsely accused Spicer of "downplaying the horror of the Holocaust." But by leveling that false accusation, Pelosi herself is exploiting the tragedy.

Steven Goldstein, a hard-left radical who heads a phony organization that calls itself "The Anne Frank Center for Mutual Respect," accused Spicer of "engage[ing] in Holocaust denial." He called Spicer's mistake a "most evil slur" against the Jewish people. Goldstein claims to speak for the Jewish people, but he represents only himself and a few handfuls of radical followers who are not in any way representative of the mainstream Jewish community. He repeatedly exploits the Holocaust in order to gain publicity for him and his tiny group of followers. Shame on them!

These over the top reactions to a historical mistake made by Spicer that was not motivated by anti-Semitism represents political exploitation of the Holocaust. Spicer was wrong in seeking to bolster his argument against Assad by referring to Hitler, and his political opponents are wrong in exploiting the tragedy of the Holocaust to score partisan points against him.

The difference is that Spicer's gaffe was not in any way pre-meditated, whereas the exploitation by his enemies was carefully calculated for political gain. All sides must stop using references to Hitler and the Holocaust in political dialogue. Historical analogies are by their nature generally flawed. Analogies to the Holocaust are always misguided, and often offensive, even if not so intended.

On CNN the other night, Don Lemon asked me if I was "offended as a Jew" by what Spicer had said. The truth is that I was offended as someone who cares about historical accuracy by Spicer's apparent lack of knowledge regarding the Nazi's use of chemicals such as Zyklon B to murder Jews during the Holocaust. But it never occurred to me that Spicer's misstatements were motivated by anti-Semitism, Holocaust denial or an intent to "slur" the Jewish people. Nor do I believe that those who have accused him of such evil motivations actually believe it. They deliberately attributed an evil motive to him in order to pander to Jewish listeners. That offends me more than anything Spicer did.

Extreme right wing anti-Semitism continues to be a problem in many parts of Europe and among a relatively small group of "alt-right" Americans. But hard left and Muslim extremist anti-Semitism is a far greater problem in America today, especially on university campuses. So those of us who hate all forms of anti-Semitism and bigotry, regardless of its source, must fight this evil on a non-partisan basis. We must get our priorities straight, focusing on the greatest dangers regardless of whether they come from the right or the left, from Republicans or Democrats. The fight against bigotry is a bipartisan issue and must not be exploited for partisan gain.

April 18, 2017
WHAT NORTH KOREA SHOULD TEACH US ABOUT IRAN

We failed to prevent North Korea from developing nuclear weapons. As a result, our options to stop them from developing a delivery system capable of reaching our shores are severely limited.

The hard lesson from our failure to stop North Korea before they became a nuclear power is that we MUST stop Iran from ever developing or acquiring a nuclear arsenal. A nuclear Iran would be far more dangerous to American interests than a nuclear North Korea. Iran already has missiles capable of reaching numerous American allies. They are in the process of upgrading them and making them capable of delivering a nuclear payload to our shores. Its fundamentalist religious leaders would be willing to sacrifice millions of Iranians to destroy the "Big Satan" (United States) or the "Little Satan" (Israel). The late "moderate" leader Hashemi Rafsanjani once told an American journalist that if Iran attacked Israel with nuclear weapons, they "would kill as many as five million Jews," and that if Israel retaliated, they would kill fifteen million Iranians, which would be "a small sacrifice from among the billion Muslims in the world." He concluded that "it is not irrational to contemplate such an eventuality." Recall that the Iranian mullahs were willing to sacrifice thousands of "child-soldiers" in their futile war with Iraq. There is nothing more dangerous than a "suicide regime" armed with nuclear weapons.

The deal signed by Iran in 2015 *postpones* Iran's quest for a nuclear arsenal, but it doesn't prevent it, despite Iran's unequivocal statement in the preamble to the agreement that "Iran reaffirms that under no circumstances will Iran *ever* seek, develop or acquire nuclear weapons." (Emphasis added). Recall that North Korea provided similar assurances to the Clinton Administration back in 1994, only to break them several years later – with no real consequences. The Iranian mullahs apparently regard their reaffirmation as merely hortatory and not legally binding. The body of the agreement itself – the portion Iran believes is legally binding – does not preclude Iran from developing nuclear weapons after a certain time, variously estimated as between 10 to 15 years from the signing of the agreement. Nor does it prevent Iran from perfecting its delivery systems, including nuclear tipped intercontinental ballistic missiles capable of reaching the United States.

If we are not to make the same mistake with Iran that we made with North Korea, we must do something *now* – before Iran secures a weapon – to deter the mullahs from becoming a nuclear power, over which we would have little or no leverage.

Congress should now enact legislation declaring that Iran's reaffirmation that it will never "develop or acquire nuclear weapons" is an integral part of the agreement and represents the policy of the United States. It is too late to change the words of the deal, but it is not too late for Congress to insist that Iran comply fully with all of its provisions, even those in the preamble.

In order to ensure that the entirety of the agreement is carried out, *including that reaffirmation*, Congress should adopt the proposal made by Thomas L. Friedman on July 22, 2015 and by myself on September 5, 2013. To quote Friedman:

"Congress should pass a resolution authorizing this and future presidents to use force to prevent Iran from ever becoming a nuclear weapons state ... Iran must know now that the U.S. president is authorized to destroy – without warning or negotiation – any attempt by Tehran to build a bomb."

I put it similarly: Congress should authorize the President "to take military action against Iran's nuclear weapon's program if it were to cross the red lines...."

The benefits of enacting such legislation are clear: the law would underline the centrality to the deal of Iran's reaffirmation never to acquire nuclear weapons, and would provide both a deterrent against Iran violating its reaffirmation and an enforcement authorization in the event it does.

A law based on these two elements – adopting Iran's reaffirmation as the official American policy and authorizing a preventive military strike if Iran tried to obtain nuclear weapons – may be an alternative we can live with. But without such an alternative, the deal as currently interpreted by Iran will not prevent Iran from obtaining nuclear weapons. In all probability, it would merely postpone that catastrophe for about a decade while legitimating its occurrence. This is not an outcome we can live with, as evidenced by the crisis we are now confronting with North Korea. So let us learn from our mistake and not repeat it with Iran.

May 10, 2017
TRUMP CAN RESTORE TRUST AFTER FIRING COMEY — OR LOSE IT COMPLETELY

President Trump's decision to fire James Comey, on the recommendation of the Attorney General and the Deputy Attorney General, raises four distinct questions. The issue is not as black and white as some partisan Democrats, and even some Republicans, seem to believe.

The first question Trump faced is whether James Comey should have continued on as director of the FBI. Although reasonable people can disagree about this, there is a widespread consensus among both Democrats and Republicans that Comey discredited the office and his own reputation by the public statements he made in the run-up to the 2016 presidential election. At that time, I called for him to resign.

He had become too controversial and too much of a lightning rod. Many Americans believe that he had influenced the outcome of the presidential election. Although no one will ever know for certain what impact his statement had on the election, the perception that he had acted improperly and may have caused a shift among some voters made him the wrong man for this important job.

My own view is that James Comey, whom I have met and for whom I had great respect, disqualified himself from continuing to serve in the sensitive role as FBI director.

The second question is whether it was appropriate for the president of the United States to fire Comey at a time when Comey was leading an investigation into people close to the president, some of whom still serve in positions of high authority in the Trump administration.

This is a complex question, especially in light of the answer to the first question. If Comey should not continue to serve as director of the FBI, then there is only one person who can fire him: namely, the president. But the president may be perceived as having a conflict of interest, since Comey was investigating people close to him.

On balance, it would have been far better for the president not to have fired Comey at this time, though again, reasonable people could disagree about this in light of the answer to the first question. Had President Trump not fired Comey, the FBI would continue to be led by a person who was no longer qualified, in the view of many Republicans and Democrats, to serve as its director. But reasonable people could believe that President Trump was motivated to fire him by reasons that suggest a conflict of interest.

Because the conflict of interest issue may be more important than the qualification issue, my personal view is that President Trump should not have been the one to fire Comey at this time. It would have been better — or more precisely, less worse — for the questionable status quo to remain than for a more questionable firing decision to be made.

The third question is whether President Trump can now do something that will make the situation right. The answer to that is clearly yes. He can appoint a more qualified, more objective, more credible, more distinguished and less controversial director of the FBI to replace Comey. President Trump's choice should be beyond any doubt and should be widely accepted by Democrats and Republicans.

An example comes to mind: Chief Judge Mark Wolf, of the United States District Court for the District of Massachusetts, is a distinguished sitting judge and former prosecutor who was appointed to both positions by Republican presidents. He has an outstanding record both as a jurist and as an investigator. He is entirely apolitical. He has fought corruption all his life and is now working to create an international court dedicated to combating corruption around the world. He would continue the ongoing investigations with fairness, integrity and credibility.

There are others like Judge Wolf who could fill the role. It is imperative that President Trump negate the perception that he fired Comey in order to undercut the investigation of those around him. Appointing a credible successor to Comey would go a long way to accomplishing this important goal.

The fourth question is whether Congress should appoint a special commission, like the 9/11 commission, to investigate the matters that Comey was looking into. Such a commission would be bipartisan, or better still nonpartisan, and would be made up of distinguished Americans with experience in investigative matters. That commission, after taking evidence, could then recommend the appointment of a special prosecutor, if such an appointment were warranted.

President Trump's decision to fire Comey can end up being the defining event in his presidency, depending on what he does next. If he replaces Comey with someone who is, or appears to be, more favorable to him and his administration, a significant crisis of trust could ensue. If, on the other hand, he appoints a more qualified director than Comey and agrees to the creation of an independent commission, President Trump could restore confidence in the American system of justice.

This decision may be among the most important in President Trump's presidency. I hope he makes it wisely.

[Addendum]
President Trump has since nominated Christopher Wray – an attorney who led the Justice Department's criminal division under President George W. Bush – to the position of FBI Director.

May 10, 2017
WHERE'S THE ACLU WHEN YOU NEED IT?

"Health care access is a civil rights issue," declared a recent email blast. "Tell your representative to vote NO on repealing the ACA." It could have come from any progressive advocacy group, but what made it remarkable was its source: the American Civil Liberties Union.

The ACLU was once a nonpartisan organization focused on liberty and equality before the law. In recent years it has chosen its battles with an increasingly left-wing sensibility. In doing so, it has become considerably more equivocal and sometimes even hostile toward core civil liberties concerns of free speech and due process.

When asked, ACLU officials are still apt to critique progressive efforts to censor "hateful" or "discriminatory" speech. If you look, you can find a page on the organization's website opposing campus speech codes. You can find instances of ACLU affiliates opposing campus "free-speech zones" and other acts of censorship. You can hear an ACLU attorney defend the speech rights of Milo Yiannopoulos and read her First Amendment critique of an incitement lawsuit against President Trump. But you will also find the ACLU attaching "trigger warnings" to blog posts.

On balance, the organization has been a quiet friend more than an active opponent of campus censorship. How often have you heard the ACLU speak out against progressive censors? How often have you seen it quoted defending speech in coverage of censorship news, like the violent protests of Charles Murray's talk at Middlebury College? Did you hear it criticize the wrongful removal of several Jewish students from a pro-Palestinian lecture at Brooklyn College? Did you hear the ACLU condemn the vilification of former Yale instructor Erika Christakis for urging students to "think critically" about rather than demand bans on "offensive" Halloween costumes? We didn't.

Instead, the ACLU responded to the Yale incident by chastising free-speech advocates for their "refusal to confront . . . discrimination and inequality on campus." Local ACLU officials offered a perverse free-speech *defense* of Muslim students who attempted to exercise a heckler's veto and shut down a speech by Israel's then-ambassador to the U.S., Michael Oren, at the University of California, Irvine.

And when the Northern California ACLU belatedly conceded Ann Coulter's right to speak at Berkeley, it did so equivocally, condemning "hate speech" and asserting that the Constitution does not protect speech that "harasses" individuals. In fact, the Constitution protects a lot of speech labeled harassment, at least by today's campus standards. ACLU national legal director David Cole subsequently issued a stronger statement disavowing the heckler's veto against Ms. Coulter, which we hope signals a new willingness to criticize student censors.

The ACLU even sided with the Obama administration's crusade against due process for college students accused of sexual misconduct. "Title IX is pretty awesome because it is expansive," declares a 2014 ACLU blog post, referring to the antidiscrimination statute. "Title IX pushes universities to do a better job of creating a campus environment that discourages and, ideally, prevents sexual violence." The ACLU has been silent about the widely documented proliferation of campus kangaroo courts that presume guilt and deprive the accused of the most basic procedural protections. (The official who oversaw these directives for the Obama administration's last four years was a former ACLU attorney.)

How did the ACLU end up on the wrong side—or no side—of urgent debates about free speech and due process? In part the organization's transformation is a result of generational shifts: The old liberal guard of ACLU leaders is aging. The new guard reflects the left's turn away from traditional liberal values toward a "progressive" politics with expansive definitions of discrimination and restrictive approaches to speech.

New generations have wrought policy changes before. The ACLU became more concerned about discrimination in the 1960's and 70's thanks to an influx of younger leaders shaped by the civil-rights movement. But for decades that agenda focused primarily on discriminatory actions, not speech, and the ACLU managed to balance the occasional conflict between civil liberties and civil rights.

Periodically its left wing, concentrated in Southern California, proposed adoption of an economic justice agenda, and periodically the proposals were defeated. Today, however, the left is the organization's center of gravity, and achieving economic justice is an explicit ACLU mission.

Partisanship is an obvious pitfall for this ACLU, as its comprehensive—and enormously profitable—opposition to the Trump administration makes clear. Executive director Anthony Romero has tried to pre-empt or defuse charges of political partisanship with an unusual statement defending the ACLU's anti-Trump initiatives, like the creation of a grass-roots "people power" project led by a former adviser to Nancy Pelosi and Harry Reid.

"We will be moving further into political spaces across the country as we fight to prevent and dismantle the Trump agenda," Mr. Romero says, vowing "to fight him at every step—both on traditional civil liberties fronts and new ones." This is nonpartisan, he claims, because the Trump administration "poses an unprecedented threat to our civil liberties."

That begs the question. Some of the ACLU's objections to the administration's policies are well-founded. The organization's constitutional challenge to the travel ban is justified by the defense of due process and religious liberty.

But the ACLU's concern for the due-process rights of visitors and immigrants contrasts with its refusal to defend the due-process rights of American college students. They can't rely on the ACLU to defend liberty and justice for all, regardless of politics or ideology. Neither can you.

This piece appeared in The Wall Street Journal *and was co-authored by Wendy Kaminer and myself.*

May 11, 2017
President Trump Did Not Obstruct Justice

A dangerous argument is now being put forward by some Democratic ideologues: namely that President Trump should be indicted for the crime of obstructing justice because he fired FBI Director James Comey. Whatever one may think of the President's decision to fire Comey as a matter of policy, there is no legitimate basis for concluding that the President engaged in a crime by exercising his statutory and constitutional authority to fire director Comey. As Comey himself wrote in his letter to the FBI, no one should doubt the authority of the President to fire the Director for any reason or no reason.

It should not be a crime for a public official, whether the president or anyone else, to exercise his or her statutory and constitutional authority to hire or fire another public official. For something to be a crime there must be both an *actus reus* and *mens rea* – that is, a criminal act accompanied by a criminal state of mind. Even assuming that President Trump was improperly motivated in firing Comey, motive alone should never constitute a crime. There should have to be an unlawful act. And exercising constitutional and statutory power should not constitute the *actus reus* of a crime. Otherwise the crime would place the defendant's thoughts on trial, rather than his actions.

Civil libertarians, and all who care about due process and justice, should be concerned about the broad scope of the statute that criminalizes "obstruction of justice." Some courts have wrongly interpreted this accordion-like law so broadly as to encompass a mixture of lawful and unlawful acts. It is dangerous and wrong to criminalize lawful behavior because it may have been motivated by evil thoughts. People who care about the rule of law, regardless of how they feel about President Trump, should not be advocating a broadening of obstruction of justice to include the lawful presidential act of firing the FBI director. Such an open-ended precedent could be used in the future to curtail the liberties of all Americans.

So let's put this nonsense behind us and not criminalize policy differences, as extremists in both parties have tried to do. Republican and Democratic partisans often resort to the criminal law as a way of demonizing their political enemies. "Lock her up" was the cry of Republican partisans against Hillary Clinton regarding her misuse of her email server. Now "obstruction of justice" is the "lock him up" cry of partisan Democrats who disagree with President Trump's decision to fire Comey. The criminal law should be used as the last resort against elected officials, not as the opening salvo in a political knife-fight. There is no place in a democracy for elastic statutes that can be stretched to fit lawful conduct with which political opponents disagree. If they are allowed to be stretched today to cover your political enemies, they could be stretched tomorrow to go after your political friends.

The debate over the propriety of the President's actions, about which I have opined repeatedly, should continue but let's take the allegations of criminal obstruction of justice out of this important debate. There is more than enough fodder for a debate over the merits and demerits of the President's actions without muddying the waters with politically motivated charges of criminality.

Partisanship seems to have no limits these days. Both parties are equally at fault, as are extremists among the public and within the media. It is getting harder and harder to have a nuanced debate about complex political issues. Everything is either evil or good. Nothing has elements of both. Actions either deserve criminal indictment or the Nobel Prize. Nobody benefits from this kind of ideological shouting match. So let's agree to disagree about important issues, but let's not distort the debate with extremist slogans like "lock her up" or "obstruction of justice." We are better than that.

May 11, 2017
TRUMP MUST PROVIDE "UNVARNISHED TRUTH" ON COMEY, RUSSIA

Within hours of President Trump's firing of FBI Director James Comey, I went on television telling CNN's Don Lemon that the key question is whether U.S. Deputy Attorney General Rod Rosenstein initiated the decision to fire Comey by writing the memo on his own, or whether President Trump directed Mr. Rosenstein to write a memo that would justify his firing the FBI director. The next day, I warned President Trump that Rosenstein "may well turn against President Trump," particularly if he were to appoint a replacement for Comey if he was, or appeared to be, partial to the president.

Now evidence has emerged, in reporting by *The Washington Post*, that my concerns may have a basis in fact. The *Post* is reporting that Rosenstein is threatening to quit if the White House continues to point the finger of blame at him for the decision to fire Comey.

As with all White House decisions, the buck stops at the Oval Office. Ultimately, the president is responsible for his own decisions, even if they were based on the advice of his subordinates. But in this case, it is important to know, as I said in the hours following the firing, whether the decision emanated initially from the Justice Department or from the Oval Office.

In either case, Rosenstein bears some of the responsibility because he knew, or should have known, that his memo would be used to justify the firing. If he did not believe that Comey was being fired because of his advised actions regarding Hillary Clinton during the campaign, then he should not have provided that cover. Now he must do something to restore his integrity and the credibility of the American justice system.

President Trump's motives in firing Comey will always remain a matter of dispute. But reasonable Americans of both parties can plausibly believe that he did not fire Comey for the reasons so eloquently set forth in Rosenstein's letter. Nor do they believe that Rosenstein spontaneously decided — on his own — to write the letter.

Only President Trump can prove that he was motivated by the public interest rather than by personal considerations. He can prove that by appointing a replacement for Comey who is at least as tough and independent as Comey himself. If he appoints such a person, he will allay doubts, at least among reasonable and objective Americans, that he was motivated by a desire to weaken the investigation of the Russian connection. But if he appoints someone who is less likely to be vigorous in uncovering the truth, he will confirm the suspicion of those who question his intentions.

President Trump can also allay doubts if he were to announce his support for an independent commission, modeled on the 9/11 commission to investigate all aspects of the alleged Russian connection, including the leaks growing out of the current investigation. All Americans should be interested in learning the unvarnished truth about these important issues.

The ball is now in the president's court. There is a great deal at stake in how the president handles this potential crisis. President Richard Nixon ended up losing his office because of how he mishandled the investigation being conducted by Watergate Special Prosecutor Archibald Cox. President Trump can avoid endangering his presidency if he does the right thing now, even if he did the wrong thing in firing Comey.

President Nixon lost his presidency largely because fellow Republicans turned against him despite his overwhelming victory in the 1972 election. The firing of Archibald Cox turned into the Saturday Night Massacre when his Republican appointees, Attorney General Elliot Richardson and Deputy Attorney General William Ruckelshaus, resigned in protest over his firing of the respected special prosecutor.

None of this has yet happened in the current situation. But fellow Congressional Republicans and even Deputy Attorney General Rod Rosenstein may well turn against President Trump were he to appoint a replacement for Comey who was, or appeared to be, partial to the president. It is in the president's interest, as well as in the interest of the country, that Comey's replacement is beyond reproach or suspicion.

Virtually all the pundits who have commented on the president's actions have either attacked him vociferously or defended him uncritically. When dramatic events like this occur, the first casualty is nuance. I have chosen, while criticizing the president for his decision to fire Comey, to focus on the future. It is imperative that the president look forward to the impact that his nomination will have on the country, on his party, and on his presidency. He did what he did, and he's been justly criticized for creating the appearance — if not the reality — of conflict of interest. The past is not necessarily prologue.

President Donald Trump can learn from his mistake and lean over backwards to do the right thing going forward. That right thing begins with who he nominates to replace Comey, and it continues with his support of a truly independent and non-partisan investigative commission.

All Americans have a stake in seeing the president do the right thing now.

Rod Rosenstein helped to create this problem. Now he can help solve it by recommending that the president do the right thing.

May 16, 2017
How Trump May Have Undermined National Security with Disclosures to Russia

If it is true that President Trump disclosed to the Russians highly classified information that could lead them to uncover the sources and methods through which this information was gathered, this could be the most serious breach of national security committed by a sitting president.

According to reports in *The Washington Post* and *The New York Times*, President Trump revealed the city from which secret information was gathered regarding ISIS's plan to use laptops to blow up commercial airliners in flight. He may have also disclosed the critical fact that this intel came from another country that is sharing intelligence with the U.S. This critical data could allow Russian intelligence to determine the sources and methods by which this highly sensitive information was gathered.

If true, this breach of national security could put at risk the lives of the source or sources currently providing valuable information from within ISIS's highest ranks. If a friendly intelligence service managed to turn a high-ranking ISIS official into a double agent, or managed to place one of its secret agents inside ISIS, that agent's life would be placed at risk.[11]

If the friendly service managed to plant listening devices in ISIS meeting places, those devices are now at risk. Moreover, the friendly agency may now be reluctant to share its intel with an "unreliable" ally who provides the information to an enemy. Let there be no doubt about the reality that Russia is an enemy, not only of the U.S. when it comes to Syria but of the intelligence agency that provided the U.S. with the disclosed information — especially if that country is in the Middle East.

Russia is allied with what's called the Shia Crescent — Iran, the Shiite portion of Iraq and the Hezbollah-controlled parts of Syria and Lebanon. Information provided to Russia may well end up in hands of these enemies of peace and stability. Russia's goal in Syria is in conflict with ours; their allies are our enemies and the enemies of our allies.

Providing sources and methods to Russia can change the dynamic in the region and cause ISIS to speed up its plans to blow up commercial airliners. That's the worst-case scenario that must be considered by us and by friendly intelligence services seeking to contain the fallout by engaging in damage control.

For the sake of our country, our allies and the world, let's hope that the story is untrue or exaggerated. That is what the White House is claiming in carefully worded statements that don't specifically refute the thrust of the story but deny that the president "discussed" sources and methods. Of course he didn't — but that's not the accusation.

The story reported that Trump disclosed substantive secrets that could lead Russian intelligence to figure out sources and methods. I hope that's not true, and it remains unproven at this time. The president tweeted that he has the right to reveal what he revealed, and Russian authorities have denied the entire account. But if it turns out to be true and the worst-case scenario comes to pass, the seriousness of this breach cannot be overstated.

President Trump may be correct in tweeting this morning that he had the right to disclose classified information to the Russians since he has the power to declassify. But having the right to do something doesn't make it right to do it if it undermines our national security.

---

11   We have since learned that the "friendly intelligence agency" that provided the intel was probably Israel.

What should be done now? First and foremost, this issue must be taken seriously by all Americans and not politicized. Democrats should not seek immediate partisan advantage from this potential national security crisis. They should work together with Republicans to learn the truth and control the damage.

Our national security agencies must consider whether to put in place, on an emergency basis, a ban on laptops on all international flights. They must put in place plans to secure intelligence assets that may have been placed at risk by the disclosures. And they must coordinate with friendly intelligence agencies who may fear further disclosures.

We must look forward and take preventive actions both to assure against repetition and to assess and manage the damage that may already have been done. The White House must put in place checks to assure that any disclosure of high-level national security secrets are not disclosed unless a calculated decision to do so is carefully made in conjunction with the friendly intelligence service that secured the intel.

There will be time enough for recriminations and partisan finger-pointing. Now is the time to stand together to deal constructively with a serious and ongoing risk to our national security.

May 17, 2017

CAN A PRESIDENT OBSTRUCT JUSTICE BY ASKING THE FBI DIRECTOR TO "LET THIS GO"?

Although the White House denies that President Trump asked then FBI Director Comey to "let this go" – "this" being the agency's investigation of his fired national security advisor Mike Flynn – Comey's contemporaneous memo suggests that it may well be true. If so, the Comey account presents a complex constitutional issue: can a sitting president be guilty of obstruction of justice for asking the director of the FBI to let go an investigation of a former White House aide?

The FBI is part of the executive branch of which the president is the head. Under the theory of the unitary executive, all departments within the executive branch are constitutionally under the direction of the president. They are not "independent" agencies. The president may generally tell them what to do. But what if the FBI is investigating the president or his aides? Does that make it illegal for the president to exercise his constitutional authority over that executive agency? That is the difficult constitutional question.

In an effort to make the FBI director somewhat independent of the president who appointed him, congress made his term ten years, thus assuring that he would serve beyond the term of that president. But it did not take away or limit the power of the president to fire him without any cause, which President Trump did to Director Comey.

Historically, presidents – as head of the executive branch – directed the Justice Department, of which the FBI is part, who to prosecute and who not to. President Jefferson insisted that his attorney general prosecute Aaron Burr for treason. He tried to micromanage the trial, granting presidential immunity to witnesses who would testify against his archenemy. He even tried to influence the trial judge – his cousin Chief Justice John Marshall.

In more recent times, President John Kennedy and Lyndon Johnson interacted with FBI director J Edgar Hoover. It is only since Watergate, that a wall of separation has been built between the president and the FBI. But this wall is built largely on tradition and internal Justice Department guidelines rather than on the criminal law.

It thus follows that when evaluating the possibility of criminal charges having been committed by President Trump – the alleged obstruction of justice – this historical context must be considered.

Additionally, constitutional issues regarding the power of the president to direct the FBI would only be raised if the facts established that anyone other than the president – a lay citizen – would be guilty of obstruction of justice in a comparable situation. That conclusion might well depend on what precisely the president asked the FBI director to do. If he simply asked the director to consider going easy on the fired national security advisor because "he's a good guy," that would not amount to a charge of obstruction of justice if the request were made by an ordinary citizen. But this request came from the president – the only person who has the power to fire the person who he is asking to "let it go" with regard to a white House aide. Moreover, the president himself may have been a subject of the FBI investigation – though he claims Comey told him he was not – and so the request may have been self-serving.

Accordingly, the fact that the request came from the president is a double- edged sword.

One edge favors the president because only he is constitutionally empowered to direct the director what to do.

The other edge disfavors the president because only he has the power to fire a director who refuses his request to "let it go" with regard to a White House staffer. Although a gentle request from the President is not quite the same as an "offer" from the Godfather, it is also not quite the same as a request from an ordinary citizen.

On balance, the obstruction case against President Trump is not strong, as a matter of law. But impeachment is more a matter of politics than law. And the political reality is that Republicans control both houses of Congress. So impeachment is unlikely, at least at this point. The best response at this time is for Congress to create an independent commission to investigate the entire relationship between Russia and the Trump campaign-administration. Only after such an investigation will we know whether other, more drastic, remedies are appropriate.

May 18, 2017
A Special Counsel Is the Wrong Way to Uncover the Truth

The good news is obvious. Robert Mueller is a good choice to become the special counsel investigating the Trump campaign and administration. The bad news is that a special counsel is the wrong mechanism for conducting an investigation that will uncover the whole truth.

The mandate of the special counsel is to "prosecute federal crimes arising from the investigation." But the accusations directed at the Trump campaign and administration are not primarily criminal. Accordingly, they fall outside of the jurisdiction of the special counsel.

Consider the worst-case scenario that the Trump campaign worked closely with the Russians to ensure his election. It probably didn't happen, but even if it had, there would be nothing criminal about it. It would be wrong and voters would be right to consider this and make them pay a political price. But it is not the role of the special counsel to expose wrongdoings — only to investigate and prosecute crime. And not all wrongdoing is criminal: coordination with the Russians is simply not a crime.

The same is true of providing Russians with secret intel that may have endangered sources and methods of an ally — Israel. It was wrong, but it was not a crime. The special counsel has no jurisdiction to investigate or prosecute this important blunder — if it occurred.

Finally, there is the allegation of obstruction of justice growing out of President Trump's firing of FBI Director James Comey and his alleged request to Comey to "let it go" with regard to his fired national security advisor Michael Flynn. None of this, in my view, rises to the level of criminal obstruction, because all of the president's actions were within his constitutional and statutory authority. But even if it were a crime, it is unlikely that a sitting president could be indicted and prosecuted for what is alleged against Trump.

Nor does the special counsel have the authority to draw up a bill of impeachment, even if one were warranted — which it is not, at least on the basis of the available evidence. That authority resides in the House of Representatives.

So what will the special prosecutor be doing? The short answer is that we don't know and may never know, because he will be operating in secret. His most powerful weapon will be the grand jury, which has the power to subpoena witnesses to be questioned without their lawyers behind closed doors. It is a crime to disclose or leak grand jury testimony (except in special situations).

At the end of his super secret investigations, the special counsel has essentially three options: he can issue indictments and prosecute the defendants, he can issue a statement that no indictments are warranted and close down his investigation, or he can issue a report.

If he were to issue a report, it would be one-sided and based on an investigation not geared towards knowing the whole truth, but rather to develop and present to the grand jury sufficient evidence to show probable cause that a crime may have been committed. The grand jury hears only one side — the prosecutor's. A report, based on no criminal investigation, is likely to be one-sided and incomplete.

It would have been far better for this country if Congress had appointed a non-partisan investigatory commission to uncover the whole truth, including non-criminal wrongdoing, not only on the part of the Trump campaign and administration, but also on the part of those current and former intelligence officials who willfully leaked classified and highly secret information to the media.

That is one issue that is within the jurisdiction of the special counsel, because it involves serious federal felonies. It would be ironic if the only indictment resulting from the special counsel's investigation was of the intelligence officials who unlawfully leaked classified information.

May 18, 2017
DON'T GLORIFY SPECIAL COUNSEL

In a rare moment of apparent consensus, Republican and Democrats, pundits and ordinary citizens seem to be overjoyed at the appointment of a special counsel. President Trump has already tweeted a dissenting view stating: "this is the single greatest witch hunt of a politician in American history!"

While I do applaud the appointment of Robert Mueller, because of his distinguished background, I worry about the process by which the special counsel investigates targets. I care more about due process and civil liberties than I do about politics. As a civil libertarian I have long opposed the way even honest prosecutors use grand juries in a manner totally inconsistent with the original intent of the framers who wrote our Fifth Amendment that provides grand juries for all federal felonies. The grand jury comes as close to a Star Chamber as any institution in America. It operates behind closed doors, denies targets and witnesses the right to have their counsel present, is presented only with inculpatory and not exculpatory evidence, and is supposed to decide only whether there is sufficient evidence to warrant a finding of probable cause. Grand jury proceedings are secret and we almost never know what happened within that black box. That's why lawyers say that prosecutors can get a grand jury to indict a ham sandwich.

The rule of criminal justice is that it is better for ten guilty people to go free than for one innocent people to be convicted, but that salient rule does not apply in grand jury proceedings. The mantra of the grand jury is "when in doubt indict."

The function of a grand jury is not to learn the historic truth. It is to learn the prosecutor's version of the truth based on the evidence that he or she chooses to present to the grand jury. Honest prosecutors, and Robert Mueller is among the most honest, will not seek an indictment of someone they believe to be innocent.

But no system of criminal justice should have to depend on good faith and integrity of individual prosecutors. There are too many opportunists within the ranks of prosecutors, who merely seek notches on their belt rather than real justice.

The real problem with the appointment of a special counsel in this case is that the most serious allegations against the Trump administration are not criminal in nature, and are therefore beyond the scope of the special counsel's mandate. It would not be criminal, even if it happened, for the Trump campaign to have collaborated with the Russians in an effort to get their candidate elected. It would have been wrong but not criminal. Nor is it a crime for President Trump to have provided classified information to the Russians that could lead the Russians to learn the sources and methods of our ally's intelligence gathering. Finally, it is probably not an indictable offence for the president to have fired the Director of the FBI and/ or asked him to "let it go" with regard to his fired national security advisor. Just because something is wrong doesn't make it criminal. To be criminal there must be admissible evidence that proves beyond a reasonable doubt that a statutory crime has been committed. It is unlikely that such a conclusion will be reached by the special counsel with regard to President Trump or anyone currently in his administration. It is possible that he may find criminal conduct on the part of General Flynn, but even that is unlikely. But even if Flynn were to be indicted it is certainly possible that Trump would pardon him.

A special counsel is even more dangerous for civil liberties than ordinary prosecutors, because they generally have only one target. That target may be a person or a group of people, but there is an inclination to find criminal conduct when the focus is so narrow. A special prosecutor is like Captain Ahab and the white whale is his target. Lavrentiy Beria, the notorious former head of the Soviet KGB, once reportedly said to Stalin "show me the man, and I'll show you the crime."

Despite the appointment of an extraordinarily able and distinguished special counsel, civil libertarians should not be applauding the decision to employ a special counsel in this case. It would have been far better for Congress to have appointed a non-partisan investigatory commission similar to the ones appointed to investigate the 9/11 terrorist attack and the destruction of the *Challenger*. Such a commission would have only one goal: finding the whole truth. A special counsel has a very different goal: deciding whether to prosecute particular individuals. At this point in our history learning the truth may be more important than prosecuting questionable cases.

May 18, 2017
How Trump Can Get Out of His Jam

Donald Trump hardly welcomed the appointment of a special prosecutor to look into the relationship between his presidential campaign and Russia—in fact, he called it a "witch hunt" on Thursday morning—but if I were him, I'd go big: Embrace the American people's hunger for the whole truth about what happened during the campaign and the first months of the administration—and who leaked what about whom—and call for an independent commission. If he truly believes he did nothing wrong, as he said in Wednesday's statement, it's the best way to prove it once and for all.

Why a commission? Because Deputy Attorney General Rod Rosenstein's appointment of former FBI director Robert Mueller as special counsel will not solve the problem at hand. His mandate is quite limited. According to the memorandum released by Rosenstein, Mueller will be authorized to "prosecute federal crimes arising from the investigation of these matters" which includes "any matters that arose or may arise from the investigation." But even if there was coordination between the Trump campaign/administration and the Russians, it is unlikely that any federal crimes were committed. Nor would there be anything criminal about the president unwisely disclosing information to the Russians that might allow them to discover intelligence sources and methods. He has the authority to declassify whatever he wants, even if it's a bad idea.

The purpose of appointing a special counsel within the Justice Department is not to learn the whole truth. The object is to develop admissible evidence against particular targets and determine whether that evidence is sufficient to bring a prosecution. There is no search for exculpatory evidence or for information that is neither inculpatory nor exculpatory, but that frames the big picture. Moreover, the work of a special prosecutor is done in secret. He hears no testimony in public and generally produces no report. If he decides to indict, the indictment is his report. If he decides that no indictment is warranted, his appropriate course of action is to simply say that, with no further comment. If he decides to produce a report, it likely to be one-sided, since prosecutors generally focus on evidence that points to guilt.

A grand jury only hears one side: the prosecutor's. Defense attorneys cannot question, and the accused – at this stage there's been no official pronouncement on who exactly that person or people may be – do not have the right to have counsel present in the grand jury room.

The role of a special counsel, like every prosecutor, is adversarial. Neither a criminal investigation nor a criminal trial is a search for truth. It may be a search for justice, but justice and truth are often incompatible. The rules of evidence – which exclude much truthful information – are not the same rules that scientists use in determining the truth. Scientists don't have exclusionary rules based on privacy and other constitutional rights.

Finally, it is unlikely that the president could be prosecuted for obstruction of justice so the special counsel will probably not get to the bottom of what happened.

If the public wants to find out what really happened, the best approach would be to have Congress do what it did after the Challenger disaster in 1986 and after the 9/11 attacks: Appoint a non-partisan investigatory commission comprised of objective experts and highly regarded truth seekers. And Trump should insist on it.

There is no incompatibility between such a commission and the special counsel; while there may be some overlap in the evidence considered, each would consider information that is not central to the job of the other. **A commission would be looking as much to the future as the past.** At the end, the American public would learn the whole truth about any alleged connections between the Trump campaign/administration and Russia, as well as the truth about the dangers to national security caused by leaks to the media from within the government.

It is crucial that everyone on this independent commission embody precisely that trait – "independence." The only way to find out what really transpired between Trump's associates and Russia is to have a probe overseen by nonpartisan – as distinguished from bipartisan – individuals who are competent, capable and respected in their relevant fields. Importantly, they must have no allegiance to either party, but display loyalty only to the truth.

People who fit this specific mold may include: career prosecutors who have extensive experience working for both Republicans and Democrats, diplomats, university professors, leading scientists, religious and civic leaders. We need people who stand for and seek the truth to engage in this process, which is sure to be complex and high-pressured, and require nuance that has so often been lacking from recent political discourse.

Precedent suggests that an independent commission is crucial to uncovering truth. Consider the Rogers Commission of 1986, which was put into motion by President Ronald Reagan to investigate the Space Shuttle Challenger disaster. The independent body, headed by former Secretary of State William Rogers, aimed to determine the cause of the explosion that took place just a minute after the mission took off as millions watched on TV. A diverse group of individuals served on the commission, including Neil Armstrong, a retired astronaut, Robert B. Hotz; an editor of a space and aviation publication, and Sally K. Ride; the first woman in space from the United States. Richard Feynman – the late physicist and Nobel laureate – is most remembered for demonstrating the poor quality of the flawed part – the 'O-ring' – by dropping it into a cup of ice water, where its rubber dented in front of a jam-packed hearing. The commission's unvarnished findings, unfettered by partisanship, were taken seriously by Reagan and led to NASA improving its safety standards.

Although the Rogers Commission was not dealing with partisan issues, the subsequent 9/11 commission was certainly dealing with issues that could have a partisan spin. One of the key problems singled out by the commission for a later review was "the fragmentation of congressional oversight over the nation's security efforts." It also dissected the role and failures of various government agencies and political appointees – clearly issues entrenched in politics. Nonetheless, the commission produced a 600-page report that led to important changes.

Analogies to past investigations will always be imperfect, especially in our hyper-charged partisan environment. But if I were President Trump, I would jump on the proposal to have Congress appoint an independent commission. If he's innocent, it's the best way to exonerate him. And even if he's not, it's the best way to discover the whole truth and not the partisan, partial truths favored by many politicians, journalists and pundits—and, most important, prosecutors.

May 19, 2017
WHO WILL STAND UP FOR CIVIL LIBERTIES?

At a moment in history when the ACLU is quickly becoming a partisan left wing advocacy group that cares more about getting President Trump than protecting due process (see my recent op-ed in *The Wall Street Journal*) who is standing up for civil liberties?

The short answer is, no one. Not the Democrats, who see an opportunity to reap partisan benefit from the appointment of a special counsel to investigate any ties between the Trump campaign / administration and Russia. Not Republican elected officials who view the appointment as giving them cover. Certainly not the media who are reveling in 24/7 "bombshells." Not even the White House, which is too busy denying everything to focus on "legal technicalities" that may sound like "guilty man arguments." Legal technicalities are of course the difference between the rule of law and the iron fist of tyranny. Civil liberties protect us all. As H.L. Mencken used to say: "The trouble about fighting for human freedom is that you have to spend much of your life defending sons of bitches: for oppressive laws are always aimed at them originally, and oppression must be stopped in the beginning if it is to be stopped at all." History demonstrates that the first casualty of hyper-partisan politics is often civil liberties.

Consider the appointment of the special counsel to investigate "any links and/or coordination between the Russian government and individuals associated with the campaign of President Donald Trump." Even if there were such direct links that would not constitute a crime under current federal law. Maybe it should, but prosecutors have no right to investigate matters that should be criminal but are not.

This investigation will be conducted in secret behind closed doors; witnesses will be denied the right to have counsel present during grand jury questioning; they will have no right to offer exculpatory testimony or evidence to the grand jury; inculpatory hearsay evidence will be presented and considered by the grand jury; there will be no presumption of innocence; no requirement of proof beyond a reasonable doubt, only proof sufficient to establish the minimal standard of probable cause. The prosecutor alone will tell the jury what the law is and why they should indict; and the grand jury will do his bidding.

And there is nothing in the constitution that mandates such a kangaroo proceeding. All the Fifth Amendment says is: "no person shall be held to answer for a capital, or otherwise infamous crime, unless on a presentment or indictment of a Grand Jury." The denials of due process come from prosecutorially advocated legislative actions. The founding fathers would be turning over in their graves if they saw what they intended as a shield to protect defendants, turned into a rusty sword designed to place the heavy thumb of the law on the prosecution side of the scale.

Advocates of the current grand jury system correctly point out that a grand jury indictment is not a conviction. The defendant has the right to a fair jury trial, with all the safeguards provided in the constitution. But this ignores the real impact of an indictment on the defendant. Based on a one-sided indictment alone, the "ham sandwich" can be fired from his or her job or suspended from university. Consider what happened to the Arthur Andersen company and its thousands of employees when it was indicted for obstructing an official proceeding by destroying records relating to one of its clients. Although Andersen was ultimately vindicated, the indictment itself forced it into bankruptcy causing a loss of thousands of jobs and millions of dollars in shareholder values. Many individual have been indicted on the basis of one sided grand jury prosecutions and subsequently acquitted after a fair trial. Many of these individuals also suffered grievously as the result of being unfairly indicted.

Consider the consequences of an indictment by the special counsel's grand jury in this matter. Not a conviction – just an indictment handed down by a grand jury that heard only one side in secret. It depends, of course on who the indictment named. In the Nixon case, for example, the president was named as an unindicted coconspirator by the Watergate grand jury. This meant that he could not even defend himself at a trial. I was on the national board of the ACLU at the time. And although I despised Nixon and campaigned for his opponent, I wanted the ACLU to object to the unfairness of a one sided grand jury naming him as an unindicted co conspirator.

So I will be standing up for civil liberties during the duration of this investigation. As a civil libertarian I care more about due process and the rule of law than I do about politics.

But many people conflate my advocacy for civil liberties with support for President Trump. I have been bombarded with tweets such as:

"Alan loves Donald. He's throwing him lifelines;" "Has he been hired by Trump? Time to come clean;" "@AlanDersh I thought you were a smart guy. After hearing you support Trumpie, guess not;" "Has Trump already hired @AlanDersh to defend him? Clearly sounds that way;" and "No matter the subject, he inserts himself in the conversation with a full-throated and nonsensical defense of Trump."

Let me be clear: I voted for Hillary Clinton and oppose many of President Trump's policies. I would be taking the same position if the shoe were on the other foot – if Hillary Clinton had been elected and she were being subjected to an unfair process. Indeed, I did do precisely that when she was threatened with prosecution. Remember the chants of "lock her up" during the campaign? I will continue to monitor the current investigations into President Trump and his associated for any violation of civil liberties. I will call them as I see them, without regard to which side benefits.

May 26, 2017

MUELLER ROVING COMMISSION TO INVESTIGATE "EVIL": A DANGER TO CIVIL LIBERTIES

Special Counsel Robert Mueller was commissioned to investigate not only crime, but also the entire Russian "matter." That is an ominous development that endangers the civil liberties of all Americans.

Federal Prosecutors generally begin by identifying specific crimes that may have been committed – in this case, violation of federal statutes. But no one has yet identified the specific statute or statutes that constrain Mueller's investigation of the Russian matter. It is not a violation of any federal law for a campaign to have collaborated with a foreign government to help elect their candidate. Perhaps it should be, but it is not. Even if there were evidence that the Trump campaign collaborated with Russian officials toward this end – and I am not aware of any – that would be a terrible political sin, but not a crime. Since the witchcraft trials in Salem, prosecutors have not been authorized to investigate sin. That is left to pastors and pundits who only have the power of persuasion. Federal prosecutors have the power of the secret grand jury, the subpoena, the selective leak, and ultimately indictment and prosecution.

That is why prosecutors must be constrained by law as to what they are authorized to investigate. Federal prosecutors are not given roving commissions to investigate "evil" or "wrongdoing" – only violations of federal criminal statutes.

Since I began raising this issue, pundits and friends have been suggesting federal statutes that might have been violated. They include treason, obstruction of justice, attempted obstruction of justice, accessory after the fact to hacking and other elastic statutes capable of being stretched to fit the conduct of any villain du jour.

But this untrammeled approach to criminal justice is fraught with danger of overreaching and selective prosecution.

The particular statutes most often cited by defenders of the investigation are among the most dangerous on the books, precisely because they are so broad, vague, open ended and capable of being stretched to fit nearly any targeted individual. Today it's Donald Trump. Yesterday it was Hillary Clinton. Tomorrow it could be you!

From McCarthyism to the failed prosecutions of Senator Ted Stevens, Congressman Thomas DeLay, Governor Rick Perry and others, we have seen vague criminal statutes stretched in an effort to criminalize political differences. Those Trump supporters who shouted "lock her up" with regard to Hillary Clinton were doing the same thing. Republicans use this tactic against Democrats and vice versa. We all lose when prosecutors abuse their enormous powers.

In the current case, the issues are more complex because there is a strong argument that collaborating with an enemy government like Russia to influence an American election SHOULD be a crime. Perhaps that is correct, though the task of drafting such a statute would be daunting. But under current statutes it is not a crime. This is an appropriate concern of Congress, but NOT of a prosecutor whose mandate should not extent beyond existing criminal statutes.

It would be appropriate for Congress to have future-looking hearings designed to determine whether new laws are needed to correct existing abuses. These hearings would be accessible to the public and witnesses would have the right to counsel. After conducting such hearings Congress could then decide whether new laws are needed, especially in an age where hacking private emails and selectively releasing them has become a political tactic. The act of hacking should be a crime, but if publishing the hacked material were to be criminalized, First Amendment issues might arise. Striking the appropriate balance between discouraging hacking and the public's right know is appropriately left to Congress and ultimately to the courts, but certainly not to prosecutors. It is not the proper function of criminal prosecutions to fill gaps in existing laws.

Another appropriate vehicle for investigating what happened during the most recent presidential election would be a congressionally mandated independent non-partisan commission of the kind that looked into the causes of 911 and the need for new laws and procedures. Such a commission would hear evidence in public, unless it were classified, and would provide safeguards to witnesses not available in secret grand juries.

All civil libertarians, whether Democrat or Republican, should be concerned about the fishing net given to Special Counsel Robert Mueller. A criminal investigation should not be a fishing expedition or a search for criminal statutes that can be stretched to fit particular targets. Partisan politics should not blind us to the dangers of prosecutors with roving commissions to investigate "matters" rather than specific crimes.

May 31, 2016

CLINTON AND TRUMP: NEITHER SHOULD BE LOCKED UP

When Republican zealots demanded that we "lock up" Hillary Clinton, I defended her against partisan efforts to criminalize political differences. I pointed out that no one had ever been prosecuted for what Clinton was accused of, and that to selectively prosecute her would endanger all of our civil liberties. As a result of defending the civil liberties of Clinton (and hence all Americans), I received hateful emails from many partisan Republicans who cared more about destroying Clinton than protecting civil liberties.

Now the shoe is on the other foot. It is partisan Democrats who want to criminalize their political opposition to President Trump. They are eager to stretch elastic criminal statutes to cover the political sins of Trump and his administration, without regard to our civil liberties.

Not surprisingly, my hate mail is now coming from partisan Democrats, who care more about destroying Trump than protecting our civil liberties.

This marginalization of civil liberties is an old story. Most people support civil liberties "for me but not for thee." Among the first casualty of partisanship is neutral civil liberties. It is only getting worse as partisanship increases. Both sides of this growing extreme are at fault.

I will continue to stand up for civil liberties without regard to which foot the shoe is on. I have no choice because traditional civil liberties groups such as the ACLU have become part of the partisan problem; they, too, subordinate civil liberties to agenda-driven political results.

Civil libertarians must oppose the expansion of already overbroad criminal statutes, without regard to who the target is. Once a vague criminal law is stretched to fit a particular target, it remains stretched and can be applied to any unpopular citizen. It lies around like a loaded gun ready to be pointed in any direction in which the political winds are blowing.

Consider the Logan Act which makes it a crime for "any citizen of the United States, wherever he may be, who, without authority of the United States, directly or indirectly commences or carries on any correspondence or intercourse with any foreign government or any officer or agent thereof, with intent to influence the measures or conduct of any foreign government or of any officer or agent thereof, in relation to any disputes or controversies with the United States, or to defeat the measures of the United States, shall be fined under this title or imprisoned not more than three years, or both."

The language of this statute may well cover negotiations conducted by Trump aides before the inauguration, when they were private citizens. The problem is that the Logan Act, which became law 218 years ago (in 1799), has never been used to prosecute anyone. The last time it was invoked was in 1803 in Kentucky against a farmer who had written a letter. He was indicted, but never prosecuted. It remains on the books as a dead letter because Congress has never bothered to rescind it. Had it been used, our prison cells would be filled with the likes of Jimmy Carter, Ronald Reagan, Jesse Jackson and many other individuals who, as private citizens, had dealings with foreign leaders.

The most notorious violation of both the letter and spirit of the Logan Act was committed by ex-President Jimmy Carter who directly undercut the policy of the U.S. government by advising Yasser Arafat to reject the peace deal offered to the Palestinians in 2000-2001 by then President Bill Clinton, who was furious with the ex-president for interfering with his policies. But no one suggested indicting Carter for violating the Logan Act – which he plainly did – because everyone knows that the Logan Act is dead letter that the law prevents from being resurrected by selective prosecution. The same was true when president-elect Ronald Reagan had his team negotiate with Iran to keep the American hostages from being freed until Reagan became president and could claim the credit for the release. Jesse Jackson has negotiated prisoner releases with several enemy counties without the approval of the U.S. government.

The reason these Logan Act "violators" can't be prosecuted is because there is a legal principle called "desuetude." Under this well-established, if somewhat arcane, principle, a dead letter criminal statute which not been used for many years, is "abrogated" and cannot be selectively resurrected to target a violator. Congress must reenact it and prosecutors must employ it, for it to return to life. This is a salutary protection against selective prosecution that all civil libertarians should applaud. Yet many Trump haters have argued that the long dead Logan Act should be resurrected, selectively applied to Trump, and then returned to its crypt where it can continue to Rest in Peace until the next political enemy comes along.

This is precisely the kind of partisan hypocrisy that is endangering all of our civil liberties. We must resist the temptations of short-term political benefits that come at a heavy cost to our long term civil liberties.

I propose a test for both zealous Democrats who are determined to get Trump and zealous Republicans who were determined to "lock up" Clinton. Apply the "golden rule" of justice – the same neutral civil liberties standards equally to both. Do not ask prosecutors to do to one what you would not ask them to do to the other. Don't try to make facile distinctions that favor your side. Be fair and objective. If you are, you will conclude that it is equally wrong and dangerous to stretch the criminal law to cover the political errors of both Clinton and Trump.

June 3, 2017

WILL 1/3 OF BRITS VOTE FOR A HARD-LEFT ANTI-SEMITE?

On June 8, British voters will head to the polls. Recent numbers show the gap closing between British Prime Minister Theresa May and Labour leader Jeremy Corbyn. When Prime Minister May called for a snap election last month – three years early – most assumed she would win easily and increase her parliamentary majority. But Corbyn – who was given odds of 200-1 when he ran for his party's leadership in 2015 – is doing surprisingly well again. He also happens to lead a party that has been soft on anti-Semitism, and Corbyn himself has been accused of anti-Jewish bigotry. When facing such criticism, the Labour leader has offered the defense that he is anti-Israel, not anti-Jewish. But Corbyn's words and deeds demonstrate that he often uses his virulent anti-Zionism as a cover for his soft anti-Semitism.

Consider a speech Corbyn gave last year where he said that Jews are "no more responsible" for the actions of Israel than Muslims are for the actions of the Islamic State terrorist group. Moreover, Corbyn's "affinity" for terrorist groups (avowed to the destruction of the nation state of the Jewish people) is also well documented. In 2009 Corbyn said: "it will be my pleasure and my honor to host an event in Parliament where our friends from Hezbollah will be speaking. I also invited friends from Hamas to come and speak as well." In light of these events, a key former adviser to Corbyn, Harry Fletcher, wrote: "I'd suggest to him [Jeremy] about how he might build bridges with the Jewish community and none of it ever happened."

Corbyn himself has said that he is not an anti-Semite but rather opposed to Zionism. Generally speaking, it is easy to say you hate Israel but you don't hate Jews. Even if this were true – and I am not sure that it is – the company that Corbyn keeps suggests that at best he gives a free pass to bigotry, racism and anti-Semitism within the ranks of his own party, and at worst, he espouses those same views. Indeed, Corbyn has been known to share speaking platforms and lead rallies with some of the most infamous Jew-haters. He has attended meetings hosted by Paul Eisen –a 9/11 conspiracy theorist and Holocaust denier who wrote a blog titled "My Life as a Holocaust Denier." Corbyn has also been associated with Sheikh Raed Salah – who was convicted for incitement to violence and racism and has been known to perpetuate traditional blood libels about Jews and said that Jews were warned not to go to the Twin Towers on 9/11 – calling him a "very honored citizen" whose "voice must be heard." Corbyn was also a paid contributor for *Press TV*, which is part of Iran's tightly controlled media apparatus whose production is directly overseen by Iran's anti-Semitic Supreme Leader.

One of the biggest criticisms of what has been referred to as the "Corbynization" of British politics has been the mainstreaming of traditional anti-Semitism. The country's Chief Rabbi, Ephraim Mirvis, has also chimed into the conversation, calling the Labour party's anti-Semitic problem "severe." Consider, the bigotry of Gerald Kaufman (now deceased), for example – a Labour veteran and close political associate of Corbyn – who touted conspiracies about Jews and Jewish money throughout his political career. When speaking at a pro-Palestinian event Kaufman said: "Jewish money, Jewish donations to the Conservative Party – as in the general election in May – support from the Jewish Chronicle, all of those things, bias the Conservatives." While Corbyn condemned these remarks, he refused to yield to widespread demands for disciplinary action against Kaufman.

Let's be clear: I do not believe that Corbyn's rise in the polls is because he hates Jews and their nation state, but rather despite his bigotry. His opponent, Theresa May, called for elections and then refused to debate her opponents. She is running a lackluster campaign somewhat reminiscent of Hillary Clinton's last year. Corbyn for his part, like President Trump, is a populist. Though they represent polar opposites on the political spectrum, they have much in common including their penchant to shoot from the hip, and their unpredictability. Many British voters are unaware of his anti-Semitic associations. Others know but don't care. The hard left in Britain, especially among union activists and academics, include many knee jerk opponents of the nation state of the Jewish people and many supporters of academic and cultural boycotts of Israel. Many such supporters favor trade and engagement with such massive human rights offenders as Iran, Cuba, China, Russia, Belarus and Venezuela. Indeed, it is anti-Semitic to single out only the nation state of the Jewish people – the Middle East's only democracy and a nation with one of the world's best records of human rights, the rule of law and concern for enemy civilians — for boycotts.

Corbyn himself has called for boycotts of Israel. He has advocated for an arms embargo citing Israel's supposed "breach" of the human rights clause of the EU-Israel trade agreement. Corbyn also supports academic boycotts in some instances, and when Israel's national soccer team was travelling to Cardiff, Wales, for a qualifying game for the European Championship, Corbyn led calls for a boycott only of the soccer team representing the nation state of the Jewish people. (Ironically, Israel only plays in this league as it was expelled from the Asian Football Confederation due to the Arab League's boycott.) Moreover, Corbyn has been a vocal supporter of the so-called Palestinian right of return stating that the Palestinians' "right to return home" is "the key" to the solution. This would soon make Arabs the majority within Israel and Jews the ethnic minority, rendering the two-state solution completely obsolete.

Whether anti-Semitism is the root of the Labour party's problem or the consequence is not important. Likewise, the distinct role Jeremy Corbyn has played in getting the Labour party to this point is not particularly relevant. The fact is that he has not stemmed the tide of bigotry and anti-Jewish hate within the ranks of his party, but has played a big part in perpetuating it. British voters now have the opportunity to choose where they will go as a nation. Will they opt to move away from stability, rationality and tolerance— and toward simple mindedness, xenophobia and intolerance? I don't know, but I hope they choose wisely.

Bernie Sanders has already made his choice. He is campaigning for Corbyn despite his record on anti-Semitism. Sanders will have to explain why a Jew is helping to elect a bigot with the views Corbyn holds about the Jewish people and their nation state.[12]

June 6, 2017
A NEW TOLERANCE FOR ANTI-SEMITISM

All over the world anti-Semites are becoming mainstreamed. It is no longer disqualifying to be outed as a Jew hater. This is especially so if the anti-Semite uses the cover of rabid hatred for the nation state of the Jewish people. These bigots succeed in becoming accepted – even praised – not because of their anti-Semitism, but despite it. Increasingly, they are given a pass on their Jew hatred because those who support them admire or share other aspects of what they represent. This implicit tolerance of anti-Semitism— as long as it comes from someone whose

---

12   Corbyn's Labour Party did not ultimately win the election, although it defied earlier predictions and finished with an extremely strong result. Taking several seats from the Conservative party, Corbyn's party finished with 262 seats, thereby increasing its parliamentary majority and influence.

other views are acceptable – represents a dangerous new trend from both the right and left.

In the United States, the Trump election has brought hard-right anti-Semitism into public view, but the bigotry of the hard-left is far more prevalent and influential on many university campuses. Those on the left who support left wing anti-Semites try to downplay, ignore or deny that those they support are really anti-Semites. "They are anti-Zionist" is the excuse de jure. Those on the right do essentially the same: "they are nationalists." Neither side would accept such transparent and hollow justifications if the shoe were on the other foot. I believe that when analyzing and exposing these dangerous trends, a single standard of criticism must be directed at each.

Generally speaking, extreme right wing anti-Semitism continues to be a problem in many parts of Europe and among a relatively small group of "alt-right" Americans. But it also exists among those who self-identify as run of the mill conservatives. Consider, for example, former presidential candidate and Reagan staffer, Pat Buchanan. The list of Buchanan's anti-Jewish bigotry is exhaustive. Over the years he has consistently blamed Jews for wide-ranging societal and political problems. In his criticism of the Iraq War, for example, Buchanan infamously quipped: "There are only two groups that are beating the drums for war in the Middle East-the Israeli Defense Ministry and its amen corner in the United States." He then singled out for rebuke only Jewish political figures and commentators such as Henry Kissinger, Charles Krauthammer and A.M. Rosenthal. He did not mention any of the vocal non-Jewish supporters of the war. Furthermore, Buchanan also said that "the Israeli lobby" would be responsible if President Obama decided to strike Iran, threatening that if it were to happen, "Netanyahu and his amen corner in Congress" would face "backlash worldwide." Buchanan's sordid flirtation with Nazi revisionism is also well documented.

Meanwhile, on university campuses the absurd concept of "intersectionality" – which has become a code word for anti-Semitism – is dominating discussions and actions by the hard left. The warm embrace of Palestinian American activist, Linda Sarsour – who recently delivered the commencement address at a City University of New York graduation – is a case in point. Since co-organizing the Women's March on Washington in January, Sarsour has become a feminist icon for so called "progressives." This is the same Linda Sarsour who has said that feminism and Zionism are incompatible, stating: "You either stand up for the rights of all women, including Palestinians, or none. There's just no way around it." And when speaking about two leading female anti-Islamists, Brigitte Gabriel and Ayaan Hirsi Ali (who is a victim of female genital mutilation) the feminist de jure, Linda Sarsour, said: "I wish I could take away their vaginas."

The irony is palpable. Under her own all or nothing criteria, Sarsour – who is also a staunch BDS supporter—cannot be pro-Palestinian and a feminist because the Palestinian Authority and Hamas subjugate women and treat gays far worse than Israel does.

Indeed, Sarsour has emerged as a champion of the hard-left. Both New York City Mayor Bill De blasio and Bernie Sanders have sought her endorsement. Moreover, Deputy DNC Chair, Keith Ellison – who himself has a sordid history with anti-Semitism stemming from his association with Louis Farrakhan who publicly boasted about his own Jew hatred– has come out in support of the bigoted Sarsour. When it comes to Ellison an old idiom comes to mind: a man is known by the company he keeps.

The same trend is detectable among the hard-left in Europe, particularly in Britain, which, at the time of this writing, is days away from an election. The British Labour Party has now been hijacked by radical extremists on the left, and is known for being soft on anti-Semitism. In a recent interview with a BBC reporter, Emma Barnett – who happens to be Jewish – Labour's leader, Jeremy Corbyn, fumbled when answering a question about how much his proposed childcare policy would cost. Rather than critique Corbyn, Labour supporters viciously trolled the Jewish BBC reporter. Tweets such as these abounded: "Allegations have surfaced that @Emmabarnett is a Zionist" and "Zionist Emma Barnett (family lived off brothels) attacks Jeremy Corbyn." Corbyn has also been accused of anti-Jewish bigotry himself. He has said in the past that the genocidal Hamas terrorist group should be removed from the UK's designated terror list, and has called Hezbollah and Hamas (which are both vowed to the destruction of the nation state of the Jewish people) "my friends." (I recently wrote extensively on Corbyn's association with some of Britain's most notorious Holocaust deniers and anti-Semites.)

Increasingly, anti-Semitic discourse is also seeping into the arts and academia. Consider the anti-Israel and anti-Jewish bigotry of former Pink Floyd frontman, Roger Waters. A staunch supporter of the so-called BDS movement, Waters has said about the Palestinians that "parallels with what went on in the 30's in Germany are so crushingly obvious." He also had a pig shaped balloon with a Star of David on it at one of his concerts. And when asked about his aggressive effort to recruit people to join the BDS, Waters blamed "the Jewish lobby" which he explained is "extraordinary powerful here and particularly in the industry that I work in, the music industry." In 2013 the ADL declared that "anti-Semitic conspiracy theories" had "seeped into the totality" of Waters' views.

Likewise, the market place of ideas on college campuses and within academic institutions has seen an embrace of anti-Semitism often disguised as anti-Zionism. Several years ago I identified the dangerous trend of academics crossing a red line between acceptable criticism of Israel and legitimizing Jew-hatred. This was in light of the disgraceful endorsement by a number of prominent academics, of an anti-Semitic book written by Gilad Arzmon – a notorious Jew-hater who denies the Holocaust and attributed widespread economic troubles to a "Zio-punch."

When asked recently about the hullabaloo surrounding her CUNY address, Linda Sarsour disingenuously played the victim card: "since the Women's March on Washington, once the right-wing saw a very prominent Muslim-American woman in a hijab who was a Palestinian who was resonating with a community in a very large way, they made it their mission to do everything they can to take my platform away."

No, Ms. Sarsour. You are wrong. This is not a smear campaign by the "right-wing," but rather, a show that people of good will reject your manifestations of bigotry.

Those who tolerate anti-Semitism from those they otherwise admire would never accept other forms of bigotry, such as racism, sexism or homophobia. It's difficult to imagine Bernie Sanders campaigning for a socialist who didn't like black people or who was against gay marriage. But he is comfortable campaigning for Jeremy Corbyn who has made a career out of condemning Zionists by which he means Jews.

The growing tolerance for anti-Semitism by both the extreme left and right is quickly becoming mainstream. That is why it is so dangerous and must be exposed for what it is: complicity in, and encouragement of, the oldest form of bigotry. Shame on those who tolerate anti-Semitism when it comes from their side of the political spectrum.

People on both sides of the aisle must have the same zero tolerance for anti-Semitism as they do for sexism, racism and homophobia. Decent people everywhere – Jews and non-Jews – must condemn with equal vigor all manifestations of bigotry whether they emanate from the hard alt-right or hard alt-left. I will continue to judge individuals on the basis of their own statements and actions, regardless of which side of the aisle they come from.

June 8, 2017

HISTORY, PRECEDENT, AND COMEY STATEMENT SHOW THAT TRUMP DID NOT OBSTRUCT JUSTICE

In 1992, then President George Walker Bush pardoned Caspar Weinberger and five other individuals who had been indicted or convicted in connection with the Iran-Contra arms deal. The special prosecutor, Lawrence Walsh, was furious, accusing Bush of stifling his ongoing investigation and suggesting that he may have done it to prevent Weinberger or the others from pointing the finger of blame at Bush himself. *The New York Times* also reported that the investigation might have pointed to Bush himself.

This is what Walsh said:

"The Iran-contra cover-up, which has continued for more than six years, has now been completed with the pardon of Caspar Weinberger. We will make a full report on our findings to Congress and the public describing the details and extent of this cover-up."

Yet President Bush was neither charged with obstruction of justice nor impeached. Nor have other presidents who interfered with ongoing investigations or prosecutions been charged with obstruction.

It is true that among the impeachment charges levelled against President Nixon was one for obstructing justice, but Nixon committed the independent crime of instructing his aides to lie the FBI, which is a violation of section 1001 of the federal criminal code.

It is against the background of this history and precedent that the Comey statement must be considered. Comey himself acknowledged that, "throughout history, some presidents have decided that because 'problems' come from Justice, they should try to hold the Department close. But blurring those boundaries ultimately makes the problems worse by undermining public trust in the institutions and their work." Comey has also acknowledged that the president had the constitutional authority to fire him for any or no cause. Trump also had the constitutional authority to order Comey to end the investigation of Flynn. He could have pardoned Flynn, as Bush pardoned Weinberger, thus ending the Flynn investigation, as Bush ended the Iran-Contra investigation. What Trump could not do is what Nixon did: direct his aides to lie to the FBI, or commit other independent crimes. There is no evidence that Trump did that.

With these factors in mind, let's turn to the Comey statement.

Former FBI Director James Comey's written statement, which was released in advance of his Thursday testimony before the Senate Intelligence Committee, does not provide evidence that President Trump committed obstruction of justice or any other crime. Indeed, it strongly suggests that even under the broadest reasonable definition of obstruction, no such crime was committed.

The crucial conversation occurred in the Oval Office on February 14 between the President and the then director. According to Comey's contemporaneous memo, the President expressed his opinion that General Flynn "is a good guy." Comey replied: "He is a good guy."

The President said the following: "I hope you can see your way clear to letting this thing go."

Comey understood that to be a reference only to the Flynn investigation and not "the broader investigation into Russia or possible links to the campaign."

Comey had already told the President that "we were not investigating him personally."

Comey understood "the President to be requesting that we drop any investigation of Flynn in connection with false statements about his conversations with the Russian Ambassador in December."

Comey did not say he would "let this go," and indeed he did not grant the president's request to do so. Nor did Comey report this conversation to the attorney general or any other prosecutor. He was troubled by what he regarded as a breach of recent traditions of FBI independence from the White House, though he recognized that "throughout history, some presidents have decided that because 'problems' come from the Department of Justice, they should try to hold the Department close."

That is an understatement.

Throughout American history – from Adams to Jefferson to Lincoln to Roosevelt to Kennedy to Obama – presidents have directed (not merely requested) the Justice Department to investigate, prosecute (or not prosecute) specific individuals or categories of individuals.

It is only recently that the tradition of an independent Justice Department and FBI has emerged. But traditions, even salutary ones, cannot form the basis of a criminal charge. It would be far better if our constitution provided for prosecutors who were not part of the executive branch, which is under the direction of the president.

In Great Britain, Israel and other democracies that respect the rule of law, the Director of Public Prosecution or the Attorney General are law enforcement officials who, by law, are independent of the Prime Minister.

But our constitution makes the Attorney General both the chief prosecutor and the chief political adviser to the president on matters of justice and law enforcement.

The president can, as a matter of constitutional law, direct the Attorney General, and his subordinate, the Director of the FBI, tell them what to do, whom to prosecute and whom not to prosecute. Indeed, the president has the constitutional authority to stop the investigation of any person by simply pardoning that person.

Assume, for argument's sake, that the President had said the following to Comey: "You are no longer authorized to investigate Flynn because I have decided to pardon him." Would that exercise of the president's constitutional power to pardon constitute a criminal obstruction of justice? Of course not. Presidents do that all the time.

The first President Bush pardoned Caspar Weinberger, his Secretary of Defense, in the middle of an investigation that could have incriminated Bush. That was not an obstruction and neither would a pardon of Flynn have been a crime. A president cannot be charged with a crime for properly exercising his constitutional authority. For the same reason, President Trump cannot be charged with obstruction for firing Comey, which he had the constitutional authority to do.

The Comey statement suggests that one reason the President fired him was because of his refusal or failure to publicly announce that the FBI was not investigating Trump personally. Trump "repeatedly" told Comey to "get that fact out," and he did not.

If that is true, it is certainly not an obstruction of justice.

Nor is it an obstruction of justice to ask for loyalty from the director of the FBI, who responded "you will get that ('honest loyalty') from me."

Comey understood that he and the President may have understood that vague phrase – "honest loyalty" – differently. But no reasonable interpretation of those ambiguous words would give rise to a crime. Many Trump opponents were hoping that the Comey statement would provide smoking guns.

It has not.

Instead it has weakened an already weak case for obstruction of justice.

The statement may provide political ammunition to Trump opponents, but unless they are willing to stretch Comey's words and take Trump's out of context, and unless they are prepared to abandon important constitutional principles and civil liberties that protect us all, they should not be searching for ways to expand already elastic criminal statutes and shrink enduring constitutional safeguard in a dangerous and futile effort to criminalize political disagreements.

The first casualty of partisan efforts to "get" a political opponent – whether Republicans going after Clinton or Democrats going after Trump— is often civil liberties. All Americans who care about the Constitution and civil liberties must join together to protest efforts to expand existing criminal law to get political opponents.

Today it's Trump. Yesterday it was Clinton. Tomorrow it could be you.

June 8, 2017

COMEY CONFIRMS THAT I'M RIGHT — AND ALL THE DEMOCRATIC COMMENTATORS ARE WRONG

In his testimony, former FBI Director James Comey echoed a view that I alone have been expressing for several weeks, and that has been attacked by nearly every Democratic pundit.

Comey confirmed that under our Constitution, the president has the authority to direct the FBI to stop investigating any individual. He said that the president can, in theory, decide who to investigate, who to stop investigating, who to prosecute and who not to prosecute. The president is the head of the unified executive branch of government, and the Justice Department and the FBI work under him and he may order them to do what he wishes.

As a matter of law, Comey is 100 percent correct. As I have long argued, and as Comey confirmed in his written statement, our history shows that many presidents—from Adams to Jefferson, to Lincoln, to Roosevelt, to Kennedy, to Bush 1, and to Obama – have directed the Justice Department with regard to ongoing investigations. The history is clear, the precedents are clear, the constitutional structure is clear, and common sense is clear.

Yet virtually every Democratic pundit, in their haste to "get" President Trump has willfully ignored these realities. In doing so they have endangered our civil liberties and constitutional rights.

Now that even former Director Comey has acknowledged that the Constitution would permit the president to direct the Justice Department and the FBI in this matter, let us put the issue of obstruction of justice behind us once and for all and focus on the political, moral, and other non-criminal aspects of President Trump's conduct.

Comey's testimony was devastating with regard to President Trump's credibility – at least as Comey sees it. He was also critical of President Trump's failure to observe the recent tradition of FBI independence from presidential influence. These are issues worth discussing but they have been distorted by the insistence of Democratic pundits that Trump must have committed a crime because they disagree with what he did politically.

Director Comey's testimony was thoughtful, coherent and balanced. He is obviously angry with President Trump, and his anger has influenced his assessment of the President and his actions. But even putting that aside, Comey has provided useful insights into the ongoing investigations.

I was disappointed to learn that Comey used a Columbia Law professor as a go-between to provide information to the media. He should have had the courage to do it himself. Senators must insist that he disclose the name of his go-between so that they can subpoena his memos and perhaps subpoena the professor-friend to provide further information. [Comey's "professor-friend" has since been identified as Columbia Law School professor, Daniel Richman.]

I write this short op-ed as Comey finishes his testimony. I think it is important to put to rest the notion that there was anything criminal about the president exercising his constitutional power to fire Comey and to request – "hope" – that he let go the investigation of General

Flynn. Just as the President would have had the constitutional power to pardon Flynn and thus end the criminal investigation of him, he certainly had the authority to request the Director of the FBI to end his investigation of Flynn.

So let's move on and learn all the facts regarding the Russian efforts to intrude on American elections without that investigation being impeded by frivolous efforts to accuse President Trump of committing a crime by exercising his constitutional authority.

June 9, 2017
TRUMP WINS LEGALLY BUT LOSES POLITICALLY IN COMEY HEARING

The "Super Bowl" of Congressional hearings, starring quarterback James Comey, ended with a number of fumbles, a few blocked kicks, no touchdowns, and a small number of first downs by either side. There will be several overtime periods, but they will be played out in the months to come. The likely outcome is a legal victory for Trump and a political victory for the Democrats.

As I had previously predicted, there were few surprises. Comey's carefully scripted statement stuck close to what he had already written in his contemporaneous memoranda. Few surprises were revealed in his written statement, published the night before the hearings. So the drama centered around Comey's examination by Senators.

Both the Democrats and Republicans have grievances against Comey: the Democrats think he overstepped his bounds by talking too much about this investigation of Hillary Clinton, the Republicans believe that he overstepped his bounds by investigating the Trump campaign, and by his selective disclosures to the media. But at the hearing itself, both Democratic and Republican Senators were respectful of Comey.

The bottom line is that no evidence of any criminal conduct by President Trump emerged at the hearing. That is not surprising, because Comey has acknowledged that the President acted lawfully in firing him, and that historical precedent — at least until recently — supported the power of the president to direct the Justice Department and FBI with regard to ongoing investigations and prosecutions.

Comey also acknowledged that Trump was right and the media was wrong, that Comey had told the President on several occasions that he was not under investigation.

The crucial conversation occurred in the Oval Office on February 14 between the President and the then director. According to Comey's contemporaneous memo, the president expressed his opinion that (fired NSA Director) General Michael Flynn "is a good guy." Comey replied: "He is a good guy."

The President said the following: "I hope you can see your way clear to letting this thing go."

Comey understood that to be a reference only to the Flynn investigation and not "the broader investigation into Russia or possible links to the campaign." Comey had already told the President that "we were not investigating him personally." Comey understood "the President to be requesting that we drop any investigation of Flynn in connection with false statements about his conversations with the Russian ambassador in December."

Comey did not say he would "let this go," and indeed he did not grant the president's request to do so. Nor did Comey report this conversation to the attorney general or any other prosecutor. He was troubled by what he regarded as a breach of recent traditions of FBI independence from the White House, though he recognized that "throughout history, some presidents have decided that because 'problems' come from the Department of Justice, they should try to hold the Department close."

That is an understatement.

Throughout American history presidents have directed (not merely requested) the Justice Department to investigate, prosecute (or not prosecute) specific individuals or categories of individuals.

It is only recently that the tradition of an independent Justice Department and FBI has emerged. But traditions, even salutary ones, cannot form the basis of a criminal charge. It would be far better if our constitution provided for prosecutors who were not part of the executive branch, which is under the direction of the president.

But our Constitution makes the Attorney General both the chief prosecutor and the chief political adviser to the president on matters of justice and law enforcement.

As Comey acknowledged in his testimony, and as I have been arguing for weeks, the president can, as a matter of constitutional law, direct the Attorney General and the Director of the FBI, whom to prosecute and whom not to prosecute. Indeed, the President has the constitutional authority to stop the investigation of any person by simply pardoning that person.

Comey's testimony should put an end to the media obsession with accusing President Trump of obstruction of justice. A president cannot, as a matter of constitutional law, obstruct justice by merely exercising his constitutional prerogative to stop an investigation or to fire the Director of the F.B.I. The President could obstruct justice, as Nixon may have done, by telling his staff to lie to the FBI or by having his staff pay hush money to bribe witnesses not to testify. But no such crimes are alleged against President Trump.

The hearing Thursday made it clear that the focus should not be on alleged crimes by President Trump, but rather on the extraordinary crimes committed by the Russian government and its functionaries in hacking the Democratic National Committee and in seeking to influence the presidential election.

The Democratic media pundits have been distorting the discussion by misdirecting public attention and false accusations of crimes against Trump. The Comey hearing should make it clear to everybody that the focus should be on Russia and on whether anyone in the Trump campaign collaborated with Russians in an effort to affect the election. I am aware of no such evidence, but this issue is so important that the investigation should continue until all the facts are known.

June 9, 2017
BERNIE SANDERS: KNAVE OR FOOL?

Shame on Bernie Sanders. He campaigned for the British anti-Semite Jeremy Corbyn, who revived millions of votes from British citizens who care more about their pocketbooks than about combatting anti-Semitism. As exit polls trickled in, Sanders tweeted: "I am delighted to see Labour do so well. I congratulate @jeremycorbyn for running a very effective campaign." There is no doubt that Corbyn and his Labour Party are at the very least tolerant of anti-Semitic rhetoric, if not peddlers of it. (See my recent op-ed on the British Labour Party and Corbyn's association with some of the most rancid anti-Semites.)

Sanders' support for this anti-Jewish bigot reminds me of the Jews who supported Stalin despite his overt anti-Semitism because they supported his communist agenda. Those who tolerate anti-Semitism argue that it's a question of priorities but even so, history proves that Sanders has his priorities wrong. No decent person should ever, under any circumstances, campaign for an anti-Semite. There are two reasons why Sanders would campaign for an anti-Semite: 1) he has allowed Corbyn's socialism to blind him to his anti-Semitism; 2) he doesn't care about Corbyn's anti-Semitism because it's not important enough to him. This means that he is either a fool or a knave.

It is clear that if Corbyn were anti-black, anti-women, anti-Muslim or anti-gay, Sanders would not have campaigned for him. Does this make him a self-hating Jew? Or does he just not care about anti-Semitism? The answer to that question requires us to look broadly to trends among the hard left of which Sanders is a leader. Increasingly, the "progressive wing" of the Democratic Party and other self-identifying "progressives," subscribe to the pseudo-academic theory of intersectionality, which holds that all forms of social oppression are inexorably linked. This type of "ideological packaging" has become code for anti-American, anti-Western, anti-Israel and anti-Semitic bigotry. Indeed, those who consider themselves "progressives" – but who are actually repressives – tolerate anti-Semitism as long as it comes from those who espouse other views they approve of. This form of "identity politics" has forced artificial coalitions between causes that have nothing to do with each other except a hatred for those who are "privileged" because they are white, heterosexual, male and especially Jewish.

It is against this backdrop that Sanders' cozying up to bigots like Corbyn can be understood. Throughout the presidential campaign and in its aftermath, Sanders has given a free pass to those who are anti-Israel – which is often a euphemism for anti-Jewish. Consider, for example Sanders' appointments to the DNC Platform Committee last summer. Seeking to satisfy his radical "Bernie or Bust" support base, Sanders appointed James Zogby and Cornell West – both of whom have peddled anti-Semitic conspiracy theories throughout their careers. Professor Cornell West– who was a Sanders surrogate on the campaign trail – has said that the crimes of the genocidal terrorist group Hamas "pale in the face of the US supported Israeli slaughters of innocent civilians," while Mr. James Zogby of the Arab American Institute has compared the "plight of Palestinians" to the experience of Jews during the Holocaust. Both men are strong advocates of the so-called Boycott, Divestment and Sanctions movement. Moreover, Sanders' endorsement of Keith Ellison for DNC Chair—who himself has a sordid history with anti-Semitism stemming from his association with Louis Farrakhan who publicly boasted about his own Jew hatred – is yet another reflection of Sanders' complicity in, and encouragement of, the oldest form of bigotry. Finally, consider Sanders' ardent support for Black Lives Matter, an organization with a commendable goal, that has promoted anti-Semitism by singling out one country for condemnation in its "platform": calling the Nation State of the Jewish People an "apartheid" and "genocidal" regime. It is clear that Bernie Sanders does not care about anti-Semitism. Whatever his motivation may be – political; ideological or otherwise – it is never acceptable to support or campaign for an anti-Semite.

Sanders has also showed himself to be an ignoramus when it comes to understanding the Middle East, and has displayed his strong bias against Israel. This may be because he has surrounded himself with foreign policy "experts" who often describe Israel as an apartheid state, and have repeatedly accused the IDF of committing war crimes. Sanders has clearly absorbed some of this rhetoric, as demonstrated in a series of infamous interviews during the presidential campaign, in which he grossly overstated the number of Palestinian civilian deaths in Operation Protective Edge, and accused Israel of using "disproportionate" force in response to Hamas' rocket attacks. Meanwhile, in a recent video marking the anniversary of the Six Day War, Sanders said: "we are now in the 50th year of Israel's occupation, an occupation which denies basic Palestinian rights while failing to deliver Israel real security." He then went on to decry the rise of political movements across the globe, which he described as "racist, intolerant and authoritarian in nature." The irony is palpable. Sanders wandered into the morass of Mideast politics only to satisfy his hard-left supporters who think in absurd packages. But he then had the 'chutzpah' to condemn political groups on the right for being "intolerant" and "authoritarian," without condemning the equally intolerant, authoritarian and often anti-Semitic, tendencies of the hard left. Sanders' hypocrisy in this instance reflects a dangerous trend in our politics: a willingness to tolerate anti-Semitism and bigotry when it comes from one's preferred side of the political spectrum.

This type of radical "intersectional" thinking was on full display in a bizarre column written by Roger Cohen for *The New York Times*:

"Elections take place in the real world; they often involve unpleasant choices. I dislike Corbyn's anti-Americanism, his long flirtation with Hamas, his coterie's clueless leftover Marxism and anti-Zionism, his NATO bashing, his unworkable tax-and-spend promises. He's of that awful Cold War left that actually believed Soviet Moscow was probably not as bad as Washington.

Still, Corbyn would not do May's shameful Trump-love thing. He would not succumb to the jingoistic anti-immigration talk of the Tories. After the terrorist attacks, he said "difficult conversations" were needed with Saudi Arabia: Hallelujah! He would tackle rising inequality. He would seek a soft departure from the European Union keeping Britain as close to Europe as possible. His victory — still improbable — would constitute punishment of the Tories for the disaster of Brexit. Seldom would a political comeuppance be so merited.

That's enough for me, just."

Clearly this reasoning of "that's enough for me" resonates with Bernie Sanders as well. Sanders was willing to campaign in the UK for the ostensibly unelectable Corbyn – who has called Hamas and Hezbollah "my friends" and has associated with Holocaust deniers and peddlers of blood libels against Jews – because he shares his socialist agenda.

Addressing Corbyn supporters at a campaign event, Sanders drew on parallels between their similar political agendas:

"What has impressed me – and there is a real similarity between what he has done and what I have done – he has taken on the establishment of the Labour party and gone to the grassroots. And he has tried to transform that party and take on a lot of establishment opposition. That is exactly what's taking place in the United States and what I'm trying to do with the Democratic Party."

"So I applaud Corbyn for raising those issues, which I think are important for my country, for the UK and for every major country on earth."

Like Jeremy Corbyn, Bernie Sanders positions himself as the socialist, anti-establishment warrior. It's difficult to imagine Bernie Sanders, however, campaigning for a socialist who didn't like black people or who was against gay marriage. Yet he is comfortable campaigning for Jeremy

Corbyn who has made a career out of condemning Zionists by which he means Jews.

Let's be clear: Sanders' attempt to downplay, ignore or deny that many of his supporters or associates are really anti-Semites should be disqualifying. Going forward he will have to explain why a Jew is helping to elect a bigot with the views Corbyn holds about the Jewish people and their nation state. It can be assumed that either Sanders shares some of these views, or is indifferent to them. Shame on Bernie Sanders!

June 12, 2017
HOW TO ANALYZE TRUMP'S LEGAL VULNERABILITY

In analyzing the issue of whether President Trump can be guilty of obstruction of justice, two distinct questions must be addressed. The first is whether Trump had the constitutional authority to do what he did. The second is if he acted within his constitutional authority, can his actions be a crime if they were improperly motivated.

The answer to the first question seems beyond dispute now, though some seemed to dispute it in weeks past. As Comey himself testified: "speaking as a legal matter, the president, is the head of the executive branch and in theory... and we have important norms against this... [can] direct that anybody can be investigated or anybody not be investigated." He is correct. As a matter of constitutional law, the president as the head of the executive branch may order the director of the FBI to end his investigation of Michael Flynn and may fire the director for refusing to obey his order. He could also pardon Flynn (as President George H.W. Bush pardoned Caspar Weinberger) thus ending the criminal investigation of Flynn.

Until recently, presidents played active roles in deciding who to investigate and prosecute. In recent years, a tradition had developed under which the FBI and the criminal division of the Justice Department were more independent of the White House. But this tradition did not and could not limit the constitutional authority of the president, especially in the absence of explicit legislation. There is no longer an independent prosecutor statute on the books, so the president retains the authority he had before that statute was enacted. It is clear therefore, that Trump acted within his constitutional authority if he directed Comey to end his investigation of Flynn. It follows from this that he certainly acted within his authority if he merely requested or "hoped" that Comey stand down. And he surely acted within his authority when he fired Comey for disobeying his authorized order or for any other reason. Indeed, Comey himself confirmed the above constitutional principles.

With regard to the second question, some have argued that even if Trump acted within his constitutional authority, he may still have been guilty of obstruction of justice if his actions were "corruptly" motivated or intended. They look to these vague and elastic terms as satisfying the *mens rea* requirement for crime—the mental element. But this is a dangerous argument that would turn the exercise of a president's constitutional authority into a crime based on what was in the president's mind. Do we really want to give a jury the power to probe the president's motives and intentions in order to convict him based on what he was thinking rather than what he was doing? Do we want the elected president to be subject to prosecution based on a finding that his constitutionally authorized conduct was "corruptly" motivated or intended? No one who cares about civil liberties should be willing to go down that dangerous road. And I doubt that those who are making this argument would be doing so if the political shoe were on the other foot—if Hillary Clinton had been elected president and the Republicans who were yelling "lock her up" were investigating the Clintons based on equally vague criteria.

There is a precedent to look to. And I challenge my critics to distinguish that precedent. The first President Bush pardoned Caspar Weinberger, his Secretary of Defense, and five other individuals who had been indicted or convicted in connection with the Iran-Contra arms deal. The special prosecutor, Lawrence Walsh, was furious, accusing Bush of stifling his ongoing investigation and suggesting that he may have done it to prevent Weinberger or the others from pointing the finger of blame at Bush himself. That was not an obstruction and neither would a pardon of Flynn have been a crime. A president cannot be charged with a crime for properly exercising his constitutional authority. For the same reason President Trump cannot be charged with obstruction for firing Comey, which he had the constitutional authority to do.

The reason that Walsh did not seek to indict or recommend impeachment of Bush is that he understood the obvious constitutional principle that a presidential may not be found guilty of a crime for simply exercising his constitutional power to pardon anyone regardless of his mental state.

Obviously if a president accepts a bribe in exchange for a pardon that is a corrupt act, without regard to motive or intent. The same would be true if he destroyed evidence or lied to the FBI. But in the absence of a criminal act, a president cannot be guilty of obstruction of justice for simply exercising his constitutional power to pardon, fire or direct.

I suspect that my critics would better understand and advocate this principle if the political shoe were on the other foot, because it is a salutary and neutral principle consistent with civil liberties and constitutional protections.

June 13, 2017
FIRING MUELLER MAY BE LEGAL, BUT IT WOULD NOT BE RIGHT

Some people close to the Trump administration have recently suggested that the president fire special counsel Robert Mueller. Many conservative thinkers and commentators have used their platforms to drive the message that the President – who has himself called the appointment of a special prosecutor "a witch-hunt" – should fire Mueller. Over the weekend, Newt Gingrich, tweeted: "Republicans are delusional if they think the special counsel is going to be fair…Time to rethink." Others have made similar claims. Although such an act might be legal, it would be a terrible mistake.

To be sure, as the head of the executive branch, it is within the president's constitutional authority to fire the special counsel. He retains the authority to instruct the Attorney General (or in this case the Deputy Attorney General, Rod Rosenstein, as Jeff Sessions has recused himself from all matters concerning the Russia investigation) to take such action. If Rosenstein refused to do so or resigned, Trump could order that the procedures setting out the appointment of a special counsel be rescinded, and fire Mueller himself under his executive authority. But just because he may have the authority to do something doesn't mean that it is right to do it. Most Republicans – including many Trump allies – have said that firing Mueller now would suggest that the president had something to hide and would be a political disaster.

To date, I have seen no evidence of any violation of federal criminal statutes by Trump. The president did not obstruct justice when he fired

FBI Director Comey. Trump also had the constitutional authority to order Comey to end the investigation of Flynn. He could have pardoned Flynn, as the first President Bush pardoned Caspar Weinberger, thus ending the Flynn investigation, as Bush ended the Iran-contra investigation. Likewise, it may well be within the president's constitutional authority to fire Mueller, although in my view, this would constitute a conflict of interest and would be wrong.

It is clear that there is a problem with regard to the president's authority to fire people who are investigating him. While a president cannot, as a matter of constitutional law, be guilty of obstructing justice by merely exercising his constitutional prerogative to stop an investigation or to fire the Director of the FBI or a prosecutor, this is not necessarily a good thing as a matter of policy. No president should fire an official who is investigating him or his staff. But this issue should be addressed not through the criminal law – which many of Trump's critics have tried to apply despite the lack of a legal basis to do so – but rather by changing the law to avoid this problem in the future. A criminal law is retrospective in nature and designed to punish past conduct that is plainly criminal in nature. If Congress were to enact a new law limiting the power of the president in conflict of interest situations, such a law would be prospective.

It won't be easy for Congress to enact legislation that deals with this specific problem without diminishing the president's constitutional power over the executive branch of government. Congress did this when it enacted the independent counsel law, which the Supreme Court upheld. That law was allowed to lapse and there are currently no legislative restrictions on the president's power in this area. Those who argue that the obstruction of justice statute constitutes a limitation on the president's power are advocating a course of action that endangers everyone's civil liberties. Stretching an already broad statute in an effort to do something it was never intended to do creates a terrible precedent. There are better ways to achieve the desired result; namely, the enactment of a very specific statute tailored to the current problem.

This won't be easy because the Constitution gives the president –as head of a unitary executive – the authority to fire the director of the FBI or a prosecutor for any reason or no reason at all (Comey himself acknowledged this.) But Congress can try to draft calibrated and nuanced legislation that would protect the American people from a president using his power to fire someone who may point the finger at the president or his staff for wrongdoing. Such legislation might well pass constitutional muster with the Supreme Court.

In this hyper partisan atmosphere, both sides are too quick to call for criminal prosecution of their political enemies for political sins that do not contain the required elements for criminal conduct.

I have repeatedly argued that a distinction must be made between disapproving of something the president does, and stretching already broad and vague criminal statutes to cover targeted individuals. It is as wrong to do that to Donald Trump, as it was to do it to Hillary Clinton. The criminal law must be reserved for willful violations of clearly defined crimes.

Preet Bahara, for whom I have great respect, tweeted an article with the accompanying comment: "Trump shld [sic] just replace Mueller with his own lawyer Marc Kasowtiz [sic]. @AlanDersh will surely say why not?" He is wrong. I would condemn such a move, but I would not immediately jump to supporting a criminal prosecution. A former U.S. Attorney ought to understand the difference between, on the one hand, prosecuting someone by expanding already overbroad criminal statues, and on the other hand, disapproving of a president's actions and trying to change it prospectively.

I do not approve of the status quo. I do not believe that a president should have the power to fire a special prosecutor, except for good cause. I write this article not to defend the president. I would write it regardless of who was president. I have also criticized Republican efforts to turn Hillary Clinton into a criminal for her misuse of a private email server. As a civil libertarian I believe that the criminal law should only be used when the conduct at issue is clearly defined – such as bribery, destruction of evidence and lying to law enforcement officials. It should not be used to fill gaps in the law, such as those that now exist with regard to presidential authority in ongoing investigations. Such gaps should be filled by prospective legislation. Congress should hold hearings on this important issue and try to enact legislation that prevents presidential abuses while protecting the civil liberties of all Americans.

June 14, 2017

OLIVER STONE'S RESPONSE TO BEING LAUGHED AT FOR DEFENDING PUTIN: BLAME THE JEWS.

When film director Oliver Stone could not come up with a plausible response to Stephen Colbert's tough questions about why he gave a pass to Vladimir Putin for trying to influence the American presidential election, Stone resorted to an age-old bigotry: blame the Jews – or, in its current incarnation, shift the blame to the nation state of the Jewish people, Israel. Colbert was interviewing Stone about his new documentary, *The Putin Interviews* – a film comprised of conversations he had with the Russian president over the past two years. The exchange regarding Israel did not make it to air but was relayed to the *New York Post*'s Page Six by a source who was in the audience.

When pressed by Colbert about his apparent fondness of the Russian dictator, Stone replied: "Israel had far more involvement in the U.S. election than Russia." He then said again, "Why don't you ask me about that?" Colbert responded: "I'll ask you about that when you make a documentary about Israel!"

If Stone's absurd response were not reflective of a growing anti-Semitism by the intolerant hard left (of which Stone is a charter member) it would be laughable. Indeed, Stone resorted to the "socialism of fools" (which is what German Social Democrat, August Bebel, coined anti-Semitism) precisely to save face because he was being mockingly laughed off stage by Colbert's audience for his ridiculous answers. Some of Stone's bizarre pronouncements included saying: "I'm amazed at his [Putin's] calmness, his courtesy…he never really said anything bad about anybody. He's been through a lot. He's been insulted and abused." Stone also expressed his "respect" for Putin's leadership. But no answer was more ridiculous than his bigoted claim that Israel did more to try to influence the election than Russia.

We know for certain that Russia (and that means Putin) desperately wanted Hillary Clinton to lose. We know that their surrogates timed leaks to cause maximum damage to her campaign. All of our intelligence agencies, in a rare show of unanimity, concluded that Russia went to great lengths to try to defeat Clinton.

What did Israel do? He hasn't said. Stone just let the blood libel hang out there for other bigots to say "see, we knew the Jews were behind this; they always are." There was an old Polish expression that said: if there is a bad outcome the Jews must be behind it. Indeed, throughout history the last recourse of desperate bigots has been 'blame the Jews.' The modern version – pervasive among the hard left– is blame their nation-state, Israel.

The reason Stone did not provide any proof of his anti-Semitic accusation is because there is none. It simply isn't true. Israel did not try to influence this election. The Israeli government took no position and its leaders were probably divided, as were its citizens, concerning the desired outcome. Prime Minister Netanyahu, for his part, remained neutral, emphatically stating before the election that he was "happy to work with whoever gets elected."

Moreover, American Jews voted overwhelmingly in favor of Clinton. To be sure, some, like Sheldon Adelson, contributed to Trump, but others, including many strong supporters of Israel, contributed heavily to Clinton. I would not be surprised if even in the face of Adelson's huge contributions, more money from Jewish sources was contributed to Hillary Clinton's campaign, but no one keeps track of such matters.

It is important to note that this is not an isolated incident. Stone's bigotry towards Jews and their nation state is well documented. He has said that, "Hitler did far more damage to the Russians than [to] the Jewish people." And then argued that this fact is largely unknown because of "the Jewish domination of the media...there's a major lobby in the United States. They are hard workers. They stay on top of every comment, the most powerful lobby in Washington." He continued to say: "Israel has f***** up United States foreign policy for years." Moreover, Stone has also stated that, "Hitler is an easy scapegoat throughout history" and expressed affection for Cuban dictator, Fidel Castro, who he called "a great leader."

Clearly, there was no legitimate reason for Stone to bring up Israel in the context of a dialogue regarding Russia's interference in the U.S. presidential election. By ducking questions about Putin and Russia, and then bizarrely accusing Israel of wrongdoing, Stone engaged in an old trope: blaming Jews – or the nation state of the Jewish people –for far reaching domestic political issues in foreign countries. Indeed, by morphing the discussion about Putin's untoward history of suppressing the press, killing political opponents, and engaging in cyber attacks against the U.S., into a polemic against Israel, Stone displayed his own bias.

The essence of anti-Semitism is the bigoted claim that if there is a problem, then Jews must be its cause. This is the exact canard peddled by Stone — and is extremely dangerous if unrebutted. I challenge my old friend (and co-producer of *Reversal of Fortune* – the film based on my book) to debate me on the following proposition: did Israel do more to influence the 2016 election than Russia? If he agrees, he will once again be laughed off the stage.

June 19, 2017
DEBATE ON CNN *NEW DAY* WITH JEFFREY TOOBIN[13]

CUOMO: The real question, legal question, important question for people following the Russia probe vis-a-vis the president is, do any of his actions amount to obstruction of justice, not investigated versus probed and what's tweeted versus what's known. We have two brilliant attorneys that are going to argue the obstruction point and help you understand what is and what is not next.

CUOMO: All right. So the latest wrinkle in the investigation with Russia and the probe is the president's legal team insisting the president is not under investigation for obstruction of justice. The president tweeted otherwise on Friday, that he was upset and wrote, quote, "I'm being investigated for firing the FBI director." So forget about that back and forth. Forget about the semantics. What about the actual issue? Is there any potential obstruction of justice by the president here? Is it even possible? There are certainly two sides to this. We have brilliant minds, CNN senior legal analyst, former federal prosecutor, Jeffrey Toobin will be arguing the position yes, there is, and Harvard Law School professor emeritus, Alan Dershowitz, who says no, there's not. I will play the role of silent judge on this, but I do have an impressive gavel. Jeffrey Toobin,

---

13   https://www.youtube.com/watch?v=cunfW_gEw0c&feature=youtu.be, CNN, June 19, 2017

you start. Why do you believe you could see obstruction in the president's action? You have a minute.

JEFFREY TOOBIN, CNN SENIOR LEGAL ANALYST: No one is above the law. That's the message of Watergate and American history at its best. The principle here is that obstruction of justice is just a law like any other and the president is bound to follow it. In 1974, the House Judiciary Committee voted articles of impeachment against Richard Nixon on the grounds that he obstructed justice by using the FBI improperly. I don't know if Donald Trump is guilty of obstruction of justice, but I do know the facts that are public now suggest that an investigation is entirely appropriate. Think about the context here. The FBI was looking at Michael Flynn, a grand jury was impaneled and Donald Trump went on a mission to stop that investigation. He approached the FBI director, James Comey, repeatedly and including in the famous Valentine's Day meeting he said let it go, let it go. And he knew, one could argue, that he was doing the wrong thing because he told everyone else to leave the room when he approached Comey. And when Comey didn't stop the investigation, he fired him. That to me suggests an investigation for obstruction of justice is entirely appropriate.

CUOMO: So Professor Dershowitz, what is your response?

ALAN DERSHOWITZ, PROFESSOR EMERITUS, HARVARD LAW SCHOOL: I come not to praise President Trump nor to defend his policies, but to defend the Constitution. The president of the United States should not be subject to criminal prosecution for merely exercising his constitutional authority in the absence of any specific statute to the contrary. The president has the right to fire the director of the FBI and the president has the power to tell the director of the FBI who to investigate, who not to investigate. My source for that, Director Comey who testified to that as well. So this is not the Nixon case. This is the Bush case. Bush pardoned Weinberger at a time when Weinberger might have been pointing a finger directly at Bush. Nobody suggested obstruction of justice. Some years ago a great lawyer stood up and opposed expansion of espionage statutes to cover what Hillary Clinton did. He talked about the dangers of expanding statutes. That great lawyer was Jeffrey Toobin.

He should be saying the same today about not expanding obstruction of justice to cover constitutionally authorized presidential actions.

CUOMO: Respond.

TOOBIN: It's – that is not what the Constitution says. There is no right to obstruct justice. It is true the president can fire the director of the FBI, but that act can be evidence of a broader obstruction of justice. For example, my favorite law professor that loves hypotheticals, what if Donald Trump said to James Comey, I am going to fire you unless you give me $100,000? Is that constitutionally protected?

CUOMO: Are you citing one of the exceptions to it which is corrupt intent, bribery as one of the witness tampering, do you believe those are –

TOOBIN: That's precisely what this investigation is about, is whether there was corrupt intent. Can the FBI – can the president go to James Comey and say I am going to fire you because you're a Catholic? That power is not unreviewable.

CUOMO: Jeffrey's point is, can he fire, yes. Can he fire for bad reason and still have the protection of the executive? Your answer?

DERSHOWITZ: Yes, the president's motive should not be probed if the president acts properly. When President Bush pardoned Casper Weinberger, nobody looked into his mind. Walsh, the special prosecutor, said he did it to end the investigation. That's part of his power.

CUOMO: But is pardoning a different level of authority than what we are seeing exercised right here pardoning as seen almost as absolute. He could pardon himself.

DERSHOWITZ: Of course. Not only that, but he could fire anybody in the executive –

CUOMO: Even for the bad reason?

DERSHOWITZ: Pardon for the bad reason. What's the reason between pardoning for a bad reason and firing for a bad reason? Once we start looking at bad reasons, we're in to Stalin and Barea, when Barea told – the head of the KGB told Stalin show me the man and I'll find you the crime. What we see here is an attempt understandably by bipartisan Democrats to find a crime against Donald Trump.

CUOMO: Is that what's going on?

DERSHOWITZ: That's what the Republicans did against Hillary Clinton. Lock her up was the same kind of attitude –

TOOBIN: It's simply not the case. That this is just like a pardon. A pardon is an absolute power and there is no motive, and the motive is irrelevant.

DERSHOWITZ: You're defeating your own case. If the motive is irrelevant for a pardon, why is the motive relevant for firing?

TOOBIN: Obstruction of justice as part of a pattern which includes trying to stop investigations, trying to stop the NSA director, trying to get the NSA Director Rogers and the head of National Intelligence, Coats, all of that is part of a larger pattern. It's not just the firing. Alan, you're focusing exclusively on the firing. It is part of a larger pattern of activity that includes the firing.

DERSHOWITZ: I don't disagree with that, but remember the president had the power to simply say to the director of the FBI, do not investigate my friend, Flynn. That's a terrible law. The Constitution should be changed, but under the current Constitution and under the absence of a special prosecutor statute, the president has the unlimited authority to do that. Just like you can't prove the president's motive for pardon, you can't probe his motive for firing.

TOOBIN: Now you're back to the Watergate problem.

DERSHOWITZ: Here is the Watergate issue. What Nixon did was hush money which is bribery, destroying tapes and telling his underlings to lie. Any president should be indicted for that, but you cannot indict and should not indict a president simply for exercising his constitutional authority.

CUOMO: You seem to be having it both ways. You are saying that you can indict them for some crimes but then you're also arguing you can't indict them for anything.

DERSHOWITZ: No, no. I'm not arguing (inaudible) you can't indict him for simply exercising his constitutional authority. If he goes beyond that, if he bribes, destroys evidence, if he tells anybody to lie, of course, he's subject to prosecution.

CUOMO: How can you say you can't go after him for exercising authority, but then you say well, you can if exercising his authority means –

DERSHOWITZ: No, no, no. It's unqualified, but he cannot – it's not part of his authority to bribe. The very act of taking money is independently a crime. The very act of lying to the FBI is independently a crime. That's not constitutionally protected. Pardoning is, firing is, and directing the FBI not to investigate is.

CUOMO: Do you accept that premise that, while you could check the president's authority, you're not in the right category of behavior to do so right now?

TOOBIN: No. I think – you know, Alan is running into – you're describing Watergate differently than what Watergate really was. The smoking gun tape of June 23, 1972 –

DERSHOWITZ: Lied to the FBI, commit a crime.

TOOBIN: No, no. It was using the FBI to stop the Watergate investigation –

DERSHOWITZ: By lying to them. That was the crime.

TOOBIN: What difference does it make? It's still corrupt intent. It's misuse of the FBI.

DERSHOWITZ: If President Nixon said, tell the FBI to stop this investigation, there would have been no crime. Maybe impeachment, but no crime. It's the lying that made it a crime.

TOOBIN: No, it's not that. It's the misuse of the FBI for corrupt reason. It's telling the –

CUOMO: Final question before we have our closings. Do you think it's wrong for the special prosecutor to look into this matter?

DERSHOWITZ: Absolutely not. It would be perfectly OK, but I think it would be better for Congress to look into it because we need new laws. We need laws to prevent the president from having the power to fire the director of the FBI, to end the investigation. We need statutes that specifically prevent the president from doing that. Obstruction of justice is too big and all liberals and civil libertarians fight against expansion of those statutes except when Donald Trump is in the eyes of the target.

CUOMO: Final statement for the audience.

TOOBIN: When the Watergate committee voted to impeach President Nixon, it was on precisely these grounds, misuse of the FBI can be a corrupt obstruction of justice. That's what this case is all about. The pardon power, the power to fire the FBI director is not unlimited. It is subject to the laws of obstruction of justice. And that's what Mueller is trying to determine, whether there was a corrupt intent to stop an FBI investigation. He's investigating appropriately. I don't know if the president is guilty or not, but Mueller is on the right track and we should all let him do his work.

DERSHOWITZ: If you allow corrupt intent to be the basis for firing a president who engaged in constitutionally protected act, today will be directed against Donald Trump. Yesterday it was directed against Hillary Clinton. Tomorrow it will be directed against other people. We don't want that kind of a vague open-ended, accordion-like criteria to be used. The difference between Watergate and this, in Watergate there were three specific categories of criminal conduct, lying to the FBI, destroying evidence, paying hush money. Here we have no independent criminal conduct alleged against the president. Everything alleged against him is constitutionally protected. We do not want to live in a country where one party can go after the elected official of the other party by using vague terms like corrupt intent.

CUOMO: Gentlemen, thank you very much. Well argued by both. I didn-t have to use my heavy –

DERSHOWITZ: I can't lose, because if my student does better than me, I get the credit.

CUOMO: You can't lose. The people will decide.

June 20, 2017
"Corrupt Motive" as the Criterion for Prosecuting a President

My academic and political colleagues who insist that President Trump has obstructed justice point to his allegedly "corrupt motive" in firing former FBI Director James Comey after telling him that he "hoped" he would end his investigation of General Michael Flynn. They concede – as Comey himself did – that the President has the constitutional authority to fire the director and to order him to end (or start) any investigation, just as he has the authority to pardon anyone being investigated. But they argue that these constitutionally authorized innocent acts become criminal if the President was "corruptly motivated."

This is a dangerous argument that no civil libertarian should be pressing. Nor would they be pressing it if the shoe were on the other foot. If Hillary Clinton had been elected and Republicans were investigating her for asking the Attorney General to describe the investigation of her as a "matter" rather than a "case," my colleagues would be arguing against an expansive view of existing criminal statutes, as they did when Republicans were demanding that she be locked up for espionage. The same would be true if Bill Clinton or Loretta Lynch were being investigated for his visit to the Attorney General, who was investigating his wife's misuse of email servers.

"Corrupt motive" is an extraordinarily vague and open-ended term that can be expanded or contracted at the whim of zealous or politically motivated prosecutors. It's bad enough when this accordion- like term is used in the context of economic corruption, but it's far worse – and more dangerous to liberty – when used in the context of political disagreements. In commercial cases where corrupt intent may be an element, the act itself is generally not constitutionally protected. It often involves grey area financial transaction. But in political cases – especially those not involving money – the act itself is constitutionally protected, and the motive, which is often mixed, is placed on trial. It becomes the sole criteria for turning a constitutionally authorized political act into a felony.

What constitutes a corrupt motive will often depend on the political bias of the accuser. For some Democrats, the motives of all Republicans are suspect. The same is true for some Republicans. Corrupt motive is in the eye of the beholder, and the beholder's eyes are often more open to charges of corrupt motives on the part of their political enemies than their political allies.

I know because I am currently being accused of being corruptly motivated in making my argument against charging President Trump with obstruction of justice. My emails are filled with such charges. The following email is typical:

"I want to know how much the Trump administration is funnelling to you under the table, of course, to keep your support of him off the record? And if it's not money, what sort pay off is it? Favors, promises, bribes... what?? Why all the secrecy when indirectly advising his legal team via cable networks' panel discussions? I think your games, shenanigans and defense of this very disturbing man give the legal profession a black eye. Shame on you! Why not come out and openly defend Trump which you are obviously doing through innuendo?

Others emails I have received include the following: "PLEASE BE TRUTHFUL. YOU ARE NOT A LIBERAL BUT RATHER A ZIONIST REPUBLICAN AUTHORITARIAN BIGOT" as well as "SELLING YOUR OPINION/SERVICES TO THE HIGHEST BIDDER!"

My motives have also been questioned by some of my academic and political colleagues. Am I being paid? Am I auditioning to be Trump's lawyer? Do I want to be appointed to a judgeship? Am I really a secret

Republican? Did I really vote for Clinton? Do I expect favors in return for my arguments?

The point is that many of those who disagree with my arguments refuse to believe that I am making them out of principle. They assume a corrupt motive.

The same is true in the larger political context. Each side believes the other is corrupt to the core. They question each other's motives. That's why using the concept of "corrupt motive" to criminalize constitutionally authorized political actions is a dangerous double-edged sword that can be used against both Democrats and Republicans by politically motivated prosecutors.

Before the recent efforts to expand the obstruction statute to cover President Trump, many civil libertarians, political liberals, defense attorneys and even judges were rightly critical of the expansive use of "corrupt motive" both in the context of commercial and political cases. But now that they see an opportunity to use this overbroad concept to "get" President Trump, many of these same people have become enthusiastic supporters of expanding the open-ended law even further in a short-sighted effort to criminalize the constitutionally protected actions of a president they dislike.

Anglo-American law is based on precedent. What happens today can be used tomorrow. So beware of creating precedents that lie around like loaded weapons in the hands of overzealous or politically motivated prosecutors.

June 22, 2017
TRUMP'S BLUFF: PERFECTLY LEGAL

Now that President Trump has tweeted that he didn't tape James Comey, the anti-Trump zealots are accusing him of witness intimidation. This is most the absurd of the many absurd charges leveled against Trump by those out to get him without regard to the law.

Trump's bluff was calculated to get Comey to tell the truth. How can that be witness intimidation? If it were, Abraham Lincoln would have gone to prison rather than the White House. As a young lawyer, he, too, bluffed a witness into telling the truth. In one of his most famous murder cases, a witness testified that he saw Lincoln's client kill the victim. The time it occurred was at night, so the witness testified that he was able to see the crime because there was a full moon. Lincoln then handed the witness an almanac and asked his to turn to the date in question. The almanac showed that there was no moon on that night, and the witness broke down and admitted that he had not seen the crime. The defendant was acquitted. Lincoln later acknowledged that he had deliberately fooled the witness into telling the truth by handing him an almanac for the wrong year. The correct year's almanac indeed showed a full moon.

I don't want to compare myself to Lincoln, but I, too, used a similar bluff involving tapes when I was a young lawyer back in the 1970s. I was cross-examining a police officer who was lying through his teeth about what he had said to my client. Pretending that my client had recorded the crucial conversation, I read him what appeared to him to be a transcript of the tape. In fact it was only a transcript of my client's best recollection about what he had been told. Believing there was a tape the witness changed his testimony and admitted making the crucial statement to my client. As a result, we won the case.

Prosecutors frequently bluff about the quality and quantity of the evidence they have against a defendant in order to get him to plead guilty or to become a cooperating witness.

What President Trump did was no different from what prosecutors, defense attorneys, policemen, FBI agents and others do every day in an effort to elicit truthful testimony from mendacious witnesses. But in today's hyper-partisan climate, those out to get President Trump will concoct "crimes" out of the most innocent behavior. This really illustrates how far things have gone in partisan efforts to criminalize political differences.

This must stop, because it is endangering democracy. The idea of turning every controversial action into a crime is more typical of tyrannies than countries committed to the rule of law. The exploitation of open-ended statutes invites tyrants to selectively prosecute their political enemies. What partisan zealots are trying to do to Donald Trump is more reminiscent of Putin, Erdogan, Castro and Chavez, than it is of our legal system.

I understand how strongly some people feel about Donald Trump being President. Many Republicans felt the same way about Bill Clinton and Barack Obama, and they would have felt even more strongly against Hillary Clinton had she been elected President. But zealotry on one side does not justify zealotry on the other. We must declare an armistice against using our criminal justice system as a political weapon in what has become a zero-sum blood sport. Criticize President Trump for bluffing, if you wish, though I find absolutely nothing wrong with it, but don't try to turn what you don't like into a crime unless you can find a clear and specific statute and precedent in support of your position.

Remember that today's use of the criminal law against a president you don't like may become a precedent to using a criminal law against a president you do like. Even worse it may become a precedent against you. So be careful what you wish for.

June 26, 2017
THE SUPREME COURT WILL LIKELY UPHOLD MOST OF TRAVEL BAN

The Supreme Court's decision to hear arguments in October regarding President Trump's second travel ban, may not itself tell us much about the likely outcome of the case. But the High Court's decision to allow parts of the ban to go forward now – even before hearing the arguments—strongly suggests that there are a majority of Justices who will uphold the most important parts of the ban.

The Supreme Court decided to permit enforcement of the ban "with respect to foreign nationals who lack any bona fide relations with a person or entity in the United States."

The Justices thus drew the distinction I have been urging since the President issued his initial ban. In a series of columns and TV appearances, I urged the president to withdraw the first ban and substitute a version that excludes only individuals who do not have a green card or other connections to the United States. The Constitution accords very different protections to US persons – including green card holders – than individuals with no legal status in the United States. The example I gave was of a man from Yemen who had never visited this country and has no connection to it, but would like to take a trip to Disneyland. Such a person has no constitutional right to come into our country and he can be excluded for virtually any reason.

This does not mean that the courts would uphold a ban that expressly discriminates against Catholics, Jews, or Muslims. But a ban that applies to countries that have a serious problem vetting potential terrorists would be valid even if all of those countries had Muslim majorities. The President has a right to focus on Islamic terrorism as a primary source of danger to Americans, and Islamic terrorism comes disproportionately from Muslim majority countries.

When Willie Sutton was asked, "Why do you rob banks?" his answer was "Because that's where the money is." Of course, not all the money is kept in banks, and not all terrorists come from Muslim majority countries. But the President has wide authority to pick and choose among countries. Moreover, the countries selected by President Trump were all previously selected by President Obama for a related purpose.

President Trump recently announced that he regretted substituting the second executive order for the first one, calling the second one a politically correct watered down version. The Supreme Court's decision shows that he was wrong, and that I was right in urging the administration to make the substitution. It also shows that many of the pundits, including lawyers and law professors, were wrong when they predicted that the entire ban would be found unconstitutional.

But it is always difficult to predict how the Justices will divide over a contentious issue such as the travel ban. The lower courts relied heavily on what Donald Trump had said as a candidate with regard to banning Muslims from entering. The Court's decision to allow part of the ban to go forward suggests that Trump's statements will not be accorded the same weight by the Supreme Court that they were accorded by the lower courts. The High Court will recognize the implications of striking an otherwise legitimate ban because of what a president said when he was a candidate. To follow the lower court reasoning, the very same ban could be constitutional if issued by one president and unconstitutional if issued by another. That is not the way the law generally operates in this country.

So the travel ban will now go into effect with regard to non-American persons. It is impossible to know whether this will have any positive effect on reducing terrorist attacks in the US. But under our law, the president has no burden to prove that he is right as a matter of policy – only that he had the authority to make the decision.

The Court is likely to find that he had that authority. There are parts of the travel ban that may face some criticism from the Justices. But it is likely that the core of the ban will be upheld.

The President should not take this as a sign that he was correct in wanting to reissue the initial ban. The Supreme Court has signaled that at least parts of the initial ban would raise serious Constitutional issues.

Notwithstanding these early signs, it is still impossible to predict with certainty what the SC will do after hearing arguments in October. We cannot even be certain of the composition of the Supreme Court in light of persistent rumors regarding resignations. But right now, if I had to bet widows and orphans money on the outcome of the case, I would bet that the High Court would uphold those parts of the travel ban that apply to persons with no connection to the United States.

June 27, 2017
TRUMP SURROGATE STARTS CRIMINAL INVESTIGATION OF SANDERS: TWO WRONGS

So now the shoe is on the other foot. A Trump surrogate has gotten the FBI to open an investigation of Jane and Bernie Sanders for alleged bank fraud. The couple has lawyered up, as is their right.

The allegations seem more civil than criminal but the Trump surrogate is demanding that criminal charges be brought. Welcome to the world of tit-for-tat criminalization of political differences. It's just as wrong to use this dangerous tactic against Democrats as it is against Republicans, but don't expect to hear the same convoluted arguments in favor of an expansive view of "fraud" from the "get Trump" zealots as they are making with regard to prosecuting Trump for obstruction of justice. Both statutes require vague accordion-like criteria, such as "fraudulent intent" and/or "corrupt motive," which are capable of being expanded or contracted depending on who is being targeted. The anti-Trumpers want to see it expanded to get Trump. And pro-Trumpers want to see it expanded to get the Sanders. Both are wrong. And both are endangering the civil liberties of all Americans.

Here is the story with regard to the Sanders. In April last year a local Vermont news publication revealed that the Justice Department was looking into the possibility that Jane O'Meara Sanders – the wife of

Bernie Sanders and former president of Vermont's Burlington College – had previously made questionable financial disclosures in order to secure a loan for the liberal arts school she headed. It was alleged that in seeking a $10 million loan in order to execute her plan of expanding the college, O'Meara Sanders inflated $2 million that she said donors had promised to repay the loans for the land purchase. It has also been alleged that Bernie Sanders – who was the former mayor of Burlington – used his Senatorial office to help move the loan along. In May 2016, after securing the loan, the college was forced to close citing the "crushing weight of debt."

It is important to note that the driving force behind calls for an investigation into the Sanders has been attorney Brady Toensing – the vice chair of the Vermont Republican Party and Donald Trump's Vermont campaign chair. In a four-page letter (with additional exhibits) addressed to the United States Attorney for the District of Vermont, Toensing stated: "Ms. Sanders's privileged status as the wife of a powerful United States Senator seems to have inoculated her from the robust underwriting that would have uncovered the apparent fraudulent donation claims she made." He continued to argue: "this privileged status, however, should not inoculate her from the scrutiny, culpability and accountability of a federal investigation." Now the Republican National Committee is circulating an attack memo against the Sanders' that is reminiscent of the attack memos against Trump circulated d by the Democratic National Committee.

Let me be clear. I don't like Bernie Sanders. He forever disqualified himself from receiving my political support when he went to England to campaign for the anti-Semite Jeremy Corbyn; when he pushed for the appointment of Keith Ellison, who had worked with the anti-Semite Louis Farrakhan, as chair of the DNC; and when he appointed BDS supporter Cornel West to the Democratic platform committee. I don't know whether he or his wife did anything wrong or criminal. But when a Republican political operative initiates a criminal investigation of a leading Democrat, my civil liberties antenna goes up.

I worry that conduct that would ordinarily be handled civilly— after all, fraudulent conduct gives rise to both civil and criminal sanctions, depending on the degree – becomes the subject of a criminal investigation for partisan political reasons. Republican zealots try to get even with Democratic zealots who are investigating members of their party. The process of criminalizing political differences escalates on both sides, and the losers are the American people and their civil liberties.

So let's declare a mutual disarmament. Let's stop deploying accusations of crime in questionable cases as the weapon of choice in the political wars now being waged by both parties. Let's leave it to nonpartisan, neutral prosecutors to decide on their own whether to conduct criminal investigations of grey area conduct based on established criteria and unambiguous statutes. Let's stop stretching already overbroad statutes to fit targeted political enemies. And let's apply the age old and salutary principle of "lenity" to all conduct before prosecuting it as criminal. The principle of lenity requires, according to the Supreme Court, that "ambiguity concerning the ambit of criminal statutes should be resolved in favor" of the person being investigated or prosecuted.

Under this principle, neither President Trump nor the Sanders should be charged with crimes based on ambiguous terms such as "fraudulent intent" or "corrupt motive." Criminal prosecution should be a neutral sanction of last resort, rather than a primary partisan weapon used to target political opponents.

July 10, 2017

COMEY DIDN'T COMMIT A CRIME — NEITHER DID DONALD JR.

Now it is President Trump who is accusing his political enemies of illegal behavior. He accused former FBI Director James Comey of leaking classified material when he surreptitiously gave a law professor friend a memo he wrote about his meeting with the president. Comey told the professor to leak the memo to the media in an effort to pressure Deputy Attorney General Rod Rosenstein to appoint a special counsel to investigate Trump. The president tweeted that this is "so illegal."

So now the shoe is truly on the other foot. Trump's political enemies have accused the president of engaging in illegal behavior, including obstruction of justice, witness tampering, extortion, even treason. And now it is President Trump who is accusing Comey of illegal behavior.

But turnabout is not fair play. Both sides are wrong in trying to expand existing criminal laws to cover the questionable conduct of their political opponents. This is a dangerous disease that has been infecting the body politic for several years now. Each side is quick to accuse the other not only of political sins, but of actual crimes, based on dubious evidence and improper, if not unconstitutional, expansion of criminal statutes to target political opponents.

Not to be outdone by President Trump, a former ethics lawyer for President George W. Bush, has accused Donald Trump, Jr., of treason — yes, treason — for meeting with a Russian lawyer during the campaign in an alleged effort to obtain negative information about Hillary Clinton. This is what Richard Painter, Bush's ethics lawyer, said on MSNBC: "We do not get our opposition research from spies, we do not collaborate with Russian spies, unless we want to be accused of treason." He said that if the story is true, those who met with the Russian lawyer should be "in custody by now."

But even if these allegations are true, this does not even come close to the legal definition of treason. The crime of treason is explicitly defined in the Constitution as limited to the following conduct: "Treason against the United States shall consist only in levying War against them, or in adhering to their Enemies, giving them Aid and Comfort." (Emphasis added.) It does not include receiving aid from a Russian lawyer, whether that lawyer was acting in a private capacity or as a surrogate for her government.

Painter's accusation is all too typical of the charges flying around from both sides of the political spectrum. Each side stretches the meaning of statutory and constitutional language to suit their partisan needs, without regard to the civil liberties implications of giving prosecutors the untrammeled power to retroactively fit the often elastic words of criminal statutes to actions that were not deemed criminal at the time they occurred.

Republicans tried to do that with Clinton by stretching the word "espionage" to cover her improper but innocent use of home computer system to send and receive emails. Comey got it right when he declined to prosecute her, saying that nobody had previously been prosecuted for comparable conduct. He then went on the criticize her — a decision that many regarded as beyond the scope of his authority.

But his critical words directed against Clinton may now come back to haunt him because if it is true that he leaked classified material, he, too, is subject to the kind of criticism he leveled at Clinton. But he, too, should not be prosecuted for leaking the material, based on the evidence that we now know.

If the allegations against Comey and President Trump's son are true, they should both be criticized for what they did. It is unseemly, at the very least, for a former director of the FBI to launder potentially classified material through a law professor in order to get it to the media. It was also cowardly for Comey to use this indirect method to seek the appointment of a special counsel. He can be rightly criticized for failing openly to seek the appointment of a special counsel. But his conduct does not seem to rise to the level of illegality, notwithstanding President Trump's hasty tweet.

The same can be said about President Trump's son meeting with the Russian lawyer if the object of the meeting was to obtain negative material about Hillary Clinton. There would be nothing illegal about any such a discussion, even if it did occur, but it would certainly be subject to political criticism.

When non-criminal conduct that is deserving of political criticism is investigated as criminal, both sides lose. Even more importantly, all Americans lose important civil liberties protections guaranteed by our Constitution.

July 11, 2017

IS COLLUSION A FEDERAL CRIME OR MERELY POLITICAL SIN? IT DEPENDS.

Special Counsel Robert Mueller will surely be looking into the meeting between Donald Trump, Jr. and a Russian lawyer named Natalia Veselnitskaya. Part of the meeting was also attended by Jared Kushner, the president's son-in-law, and Paul Manafort, who at the time was running Trump's campaign. It is now seems clear from the emails that the Trump people went to the meeting expecting to be given dirt on Hillary Clinton from the Russian government. The question remains, if this is all true, is it criminal?

The first issue that must be addressed by Mueller is whether any existing criminal statutes would be violated by collusion between a campaign and a foreign government, if such collusion were to be proved? Unless there is a clear violation of an existing criminal statute, there would be no crime. Obviously, if anyone conspired in advance with another to commit a crime, such as hacking the DNC, that would be criminal. But merely seeking to obtain the work product of a prior hack would be no more criminal than a newspaper publishing the work product of thefts such as the Pentagon Papers and the material stolen by Snowden and Manning. Moreover, the emails sent to Trump Jr. say that the dirt peddled by Veselnitskaya came from "official documents." No mention is made of hacking or other illegal activities. So it is unlikely that attendance at the meeting violated any criminal statute.

Whether or not such collusion, if it occurred, is a crime, it is clear that the American people have the right to know whether any sort of collusion – legal or illegal – took place. And, if so, what was its nature.

The Mueller investigation is limited to possible <u>criminal</u> activity. Probing the moral, political, or other non-criminal implications of collusion with, or interference by, Russia is beyond the jurisdiction of the Special Counsel. It is the role of Congress, not the Criminal Division of the Justice Department, to make changes in existing laws. Perhaps mere collusion by a campaign with a foreign government <u>should be made</u> a crime, so as to prevent <u>future</u> contamination of our elections. But it is not <u>currently</u> a crime.

Nor will it be easy to draft a criminal statute prohibiting a campaign from using material provided by a foreign power, without trenching on the Constitutional rights of candidates. But this is all up to Congress and the courts, not the Special Counsel, with his limited jurisdiction.

That is why the entire issue of alleged collusion with, and interference by, the Russians should be investigated openly by an independent non-partisan commission, rather than by a prosecutor behind the closed doors of a grand jury. The end result of a secret grand jury investigation will be an up or down determination whether to indict or not to indict. If there are no indictments, that will end the matter. The Special Counsel may issue a report summarizing the results of his investigation, but many experts believe that such reports are improper, since the subjects of the investigation do not have the right to present exculpatory evidence to the grand jury, which typically hears only one side of the case. Beyond any report, there will also be selection leaks, such as the many that already occurred. Leaks, too, tend to be one-sided and agenda driven.

A public non-partisan commission investigation, or even one conducted by partisans in Congress, would be open for the most part. They would hear all sides of the story, and the public would be able to judge for itself whether there was improper collusion. A Commission or

Congressional Committee could also recommend changes in the law for the future.

The American people need to know precisely what the Russians tried to do and did, and what, if anything, the Trump campaign knew and did. These issues go beyond a cops-and-robber whodunit. They involve the very essence of our democracy.

CONCLUSION

Donald Trump is likely to remain president until the end of his term or terms. Despite the ongoing criminal and congressional investigations, he is unlikely to be prosecuted, impeached or forced to resign. The evidence currently in the public domain provides no basis for the extreme sanctions being sought by partisan extremists, some in the media and several academics. This does not mean that calls for Trump's removal from office will not persist. They will, because they are a prime weapon in the war being conducted to weaken the Trump presidency and prevent the President from carrying out his agenda. If this battle plan seems familiar, it is because it was originally drawn up by Republicans who directed it against President Bill Clinton.

The Republicans who engineered Clinton's impeachment – following a massive investigation that produced evidence of sexual sins rather than political or economic crimes – realized that they did not have the votes to have Clinton removed, or the evidence to have him prosecuted (if that was even possible under the constitution.) But there was enough smoke – much of it generated by Clinton's own non-criminal misconduct and the God-awful advice he received from his initial lawyer[14] – to keep Clinton preoccupied during much of his second term.

The Democrats will try to do to President Trump what the Republicans did to President Clinton. It is too early to tell whether they will succeed. Moreover, there are other dynamics at play, including a fragmented Republican party, whose congressional leaders do not always see eye to eye with their president. What is not too early to know is that the Democrats will do everything in their power to exploit every misstep the President has taken in the past and will take in the future. That is the nature of contemporary hyper-partisan politics.

What is also too early to know is whether more or different evidence will emerge against members of the Trump administration as a result

---

14   Robert Bennett advised him against paying damages to Paula Jones, which would have ended the lawsuit and the subsequent deposition that led to Clinton's impeachment and disbarment. See Dershowitz, Sexual McCarthyism.

of the ongoing investigations. Recall that with virtually all previous investigations of presidents, evidence emerged of criminal or unethical conduct that was not part of the original mandate.

We know that General Michael Flynn is actually seeking a deal from special counsel Robert Mueller. What we don't know is whether he has anything to offer against President Trump or members of his administration in exchange for receiving immunity.

When I taught criminal law and constitutional procedure at Harvard Law School for fifty years, I told my students that, "the first rule for committing crimes in America is, 'always commit the crime with someone more important than you.'" The reason is that you can trade testimony against the more important person for your own "get out of jail" card. The problem for some potential dealmakers is that they don't have anything to offer against the more important person. So instead of just "singing," these mendacious witnesses "compose" as well. They make up – and exaggerate – incriminating stories against "Mr. Big" in order to save their own rear ends.

There is no evidence that this is happening in the current investigation, though there is always the possibility that it will. It is unlikely that members of the Trump family, who are now under scrutiny, will turn against the President. There is also the possibility that new evidence of past criminal or impeachable conduct may legitimately emerge from the Mueller investigation, or that such conduct may be committed in the future. That is why so many of my liberal friends and colleagues insist on keeping the pressure on the Trump administration and its leader. For anti-Trump zealots, this is a win-win strategy: if new evidence of criminality emerges, they win; but even if there is no evidence, the pressure alone will slow down what they understandably regard as policies that are dangerous to America and the world. In the end a balance must be struck that recognizes both the dangers of some Trump policies, and the dangers of some of the tactics being used to slow them down. And that is why this is a work in progress. Stay tuned. No one knows how the story will end, but with Donald Trump as president we can be certain that it will never be boring.

ACKNOWLEDGEMENTS

This book could not have been completed so quickly without the assistance of my paralegal Gabrielle Debinski and my assistant Maura Kelley. My agent Karen Gantz facilitated the publication. Friends and relatives who reviewed and improved portions of the draft include my wife Carolyn Cohen, my son Elon, my associate Aaron Voloj Dessauer, my friends Michael Miller and Harvey Silverglate, and several others who know who they are. Because of the controversial nature of this book, I want to be clear that the ideas are mine and no else should be held responsible for them.

ABOUT THE AUTHOR

Professor Alan M. Dershowitz is one of the nation's "most distinguished defenders of individual rights." He is Felix Frankfurter Professor of Law Emeritus at Harvard Law School, and author of twenty-five works including *The New York Times* #1 bestseller *Chutzpah*.

DATE DUE

This item is Due on
or before Date shown.

JAN - - 2018

Made in the USA
Lexington, KY
21 December 2017